Tom's Collection

Cosmic Lessons

Holly Fourchalk & Tom

Also By Holly Fourchalk

Adrenal Fatigue: Why am I so tired all the time?

Are you what you eat? Why Your Intestines Are The Foundation of Good Health

Cancer: Why what you don't know about your treatment could harm you.

Depression: The Real Cause May Be Your Body.

Diabetes: What Your Physician Doesn't Know

Glutathione: Your Body's Secret Healing Agent

Your Heart: Are you taking care of it?

Inflammation: The Silent Killer

Managing Your Weight: Why your body may be working against you and what you can do about it.

The Chocolate Controversy: The Bad, the Mediocre and the Awesome

So What's the Point: If You Have Ever Asked

Your Immune System: Is Yours Protecting You?

Your Vital Liver: How to protect your liver from life's toxins

The Entwined Collection

Entwined: A Romantic Journey Back into Health

Entwined: The Ongoing Journey

Tom's Collection

The Cosmic Socialite

Comic Healing

All of the above are available at DrHollyBooks.com

Tom's Collection

Cosmic Lessons

Holly Fourchalk & Tom

Copyright 2018 © Holly Fourchalk

All rights reserved. No part of this publication may be reproduced or transmitted in any form or by any means without prior written permission of the author, except by a reviewer who may quote brief passages in a review.

Cover design by Peter Forde. Published by Leah Albrecht.

Choices Unlimited for Health & Wellness
Dr. Holly Fourchalk, Ph.D., DNM®, RHT, HT
Tel: 604.764.5203
Websites: ChoicesUnlimited.ca & DrHollyBooks.com
E-mail: holly@choicesunlimited.ca

ISBN 978-1-989420-02-7 (softcover)
ISBN 978-1-989420-03-4 (ebook)

Disclaimer

Tom does not claim to be a Master. But he has an agenda. He wants people to grow and learn, heal and prepare for more. As such he wanted to write this book.

He gave me the chapter headings and told me conceptually what he wanted each chapter to be about. A couple of times, he came to me and said I went off on the wrong track. So, I had to go back and re-write the chapter.

As such, I am just the messenger.

To Tom, My Love, an awe-inspiring person, both on this side and the other side

To my parents who loved Tom dearly

To all my friends and my family who provided so much support through a difficult and challenging journey

Table of Contents

1. Introduction 1
2. Relationships Across Dimensions 10
3. What is a Soul Mate? 41
4. Forgiveness 48
5. There is No Judgement 54
6. Purpose 57
7. Fears Can Get in the Way 64
8. Being Good Enough 70
9. Engaging in the Lessons 76
10. How Do We Learn on the Other Side? 83
11. Choices 89
12. Learning to Own Your Stuff, Not Theirs 95
13. Learning to Just Be 104
14. Emotions on the Other Side 106
15. Lessons About Healing 113
16. What We Take with Us 117
17. What we Learn on the Other Side 123
18. Connecting with the Other Side 127
19. Come from a Place of Abundance 136
20. Learning to Trust the Self 140
21. Givers and Takers 145
22. Moving Between Dimensions 153

23. Awareness 162
24. Dying, Death and Dead 165
25. Energies, Frequencies and Vibrations 171
26. Portals 175
27. Can One Soul Occupy Two Bodies Simultaneously 179
28. When You Ask, Wait for the Answers 183
29. What is Love 185
30. Attachment 193
31. We Can Work with Those on the Other Side 200
32. Can They Work with More than One Person on this Side? 202
Afterward 209

Chapter 1

Introduction

This is the third book in Tom Collection series. I have no idea how many books there will be, as I am not in charge. Tom is. Tom is a wonderful soul who really developed spiritually during the last several years of his life. When he crossed over to the other side, he took great strides in his own continuing development and found a way to share that with me.

Tom and I became very good friends over a number of years and then became romantic partners. During that time, we explored a lot of esoteric concepts and philosophies; went to a wide variety of courses and programs; and played with a number of different esoteric exercises.

While both on this side, I don't think either of us expected that when one of us crossed over, our relationship would continue. But it did. Right from the first day, I could "feel" Tom. I could "feel" him hug me during the day and cuddle me at night. In fact, he woke me up several times a night. It was both very comforting and very disconcerting at the same time.

When I told people he was there, I think they thought he was "there in spirit" not realizing how much I could actually "feel" him.

The first book "we" wrote, was about Tom's journey on the other side. Or more specifically, my experience of Tom on other side; my self doubt and self questioning; as well as many of Tom's connections with family and friends on this side as he continued to learn how to connect. As Tom's capacities and skills developed on the other side, he also taught me to "hear" and then to "see" him.

Thus, began the most extraordinary journey of my life. Well at least of this life, as I have no recall of other lives. Tom and I had both had fun going to "psychics" over the years, both together and individually, who claimed that we did have many past lives together. But neither of us had any recall of them when on this side.

Meanwhile, on the other side, Tom is becoming more and more "aware". He claims he is aware of our other lives, both together and apart. As I said, at this point, I still have no recall of those lives, however, we have been told several times that we were in several lives together and in a more recent one, we had a very good marriage.

Tom also claims that the programs, exercises, discussions, etc. we engaged in together, not only provided us with growth and understanding but healing and preparation, on several different levels, that we were not consciously aware of. He claims that it is because of the work we did, in this lifetime and in others, that we are now able to keep the relationship going or to develop it across the dimensions.

During the first part of our *new* journey together, I started going to see psychics, mediums, channelers, etc. to determine if I was creating all of this, in my mind, as a very creative way to work through grieving or if it was "really" happening.

One of the most potent early experiences, after Tom crossed over, was attending a meeting, "Messages from the Other Side" with two mediums.

Suzanna, a good friend of Tom and myself went in and signed up for the 7PM presentation, reserved our seats in the front row and then went for dinner. Dinner was slow in coming, so we came back late. But we still had our front row seats. There were 35 in the audience.

They started by explaining what the difference was between a medium and a psychic. They claimed that they did not tell you your future or your past but rather simply conveyed messages from the other side. They were not there to analyze or interpret the message, but rather to simply convey it. Having never attended anything like that before, I simply wondered if I would get a message from Tom.

The prior night, I had gone to a place where Tom and I liked to go and meditate, when he was on this side. It was in a beautiful forested area up on a mountain with gorgeous trees and lush underground. I meditated for awhile and had a one-way conversation with Tom. I explained what Suzanna and I were doing the next day and asked him to be there. I told him I needed him to answer three questions for me, so that I had a validation or a confirmation that it really was him and not just my mind being creative.

So now, Suzanna and I were here, in the room, with 35 others. One of the two mediums would walk up to a person and ask if she could talk with you. They didn't "know us from Adam"; they didn't have our names or birthdates or anything. Yet they provided incredibly specific, detailed and accurate information for most of the people in the room, including us.

First, one of the ladies came up to me, she had looked at me repeatedly, and I was concerned that there was something wrong. When I nodded yes that she could talk with me, she stated that my mother had recently crossed over and that she was sending love and healing to my father and myself. *My mother had crossed over just three weeks prior to Tom and my father was still with me.*

Then the two women looked at me and together stated that I had a lot of guides working with me…then

- *(Psychics) Your husband is coming in strong…he really loves you…like he really loves you.*

That was huge for me. I tried to keep a neutral face, but the tears started to roll down my face. S**t, I didn't want to give any information away, verbal or facial.

The ladies both started talking to me. I was the only one that both of them talked too. I have no idea why or what that meant, if anything. But they continued on, saying that my house had just sold. Yup, I had signed the papers four hours before! They talked about how Tom had crossed over and that it was really recent. Yup three weeks before! They claimed he wanted to write a book with me. In between their comments they repeatedly told me how much he loved me and how important it was for me to know that.

One of them talked about how I could connect with him more. Then she started to laugh saying, that he was always there with me, I just needed to reach out and allow the awareness of it. Really? I really wanted to believe that!

But then I silently questioned to myself whether this was just a basic concept that psychics/mediums told their clients. However, when I heard them talk to other people in similar situations, their messages were entirely different.

Terry, one of the psychics, somewhat addressed the questions I asked Tom to address the night before. At the end of the session, she came over and kneeled in front of me. She said that said she was supposed to be answering three questions but that they were too complicated. She told me that if I emailed her, she would give me better answers. I still hadn't said a word!

I had already connected with two other mediums before that evening. One by phone, whom Tom and I had connected with, when we were just friends. Both in the first session, years before, and in this second session, Jane gave a lot of detailed history about Tom.

The relationship between him and his father while growing up and as a young man wherein he had been very abused, physically and verbally. She also gave a lot of detail on his prior marriage which had also been very emotionally abusive.

In this second session, Jane started talking about the relationship between Tom and I and the issues that we had helped one another with; about what a deep profound love we had; that our relationship would continue to grow with him on the other side; and that he would help me develop "my gifts". She kept reinforcing how sorry he was that he had left and again, how much he loved me.

A friend then connected me with another medium. An elderly lady, Mary, who had a lot of training from many "Masters" and who didn't charge anything! She also kept talking about how much Tom loved me and how sorry he was that he left me. She claimed that both he and my mother were bathing me in so much love and healing; but that Tom was much stronger and again, that he *really* loved me. Again, that Tom was going to work with me from the other side. And again, that our love would grow stronger. It was becoming a repeating theme.

Of course, my analytical sceptical mind kept questioning, if that was the type of thing, they told everyone.

The experiences with Tom increased, not just with me, but with family and friends. Tom had a profound affect on my Dad when he showed up visually and stayed for some time. My Dad phoned me right afterwards and although he is 87 years old, he was as excited as a teenager. Dad claimed that Tom hadn't said anything but had a look on his face as if to say, "See Pops, I can do it!" Tom also connected with our Realtor and the General Contractor who was building the new house. He solved problems for the General Contractor not only with our house but with another house he was building. The General Contractor said, "Your house was the fastest I have ever built, whether bigger or smaller, thanks to you and Tom!"

Tom's capacity to connect with me certainly developed, and my capacity to hear and see him also developed. The first book, Tom: Cosmic Socialite, was about how that first part of the journey evolved.

Then Tom started to teach me about healing in ways I had never heard about. I had gone to med school and naturopathic college; I had PhDs in psychology and in nutrition and a Dr of Natural Medicine; I had a Masters in Herbal Medicine; was an Advanced Ayurvedic practitioner; and held a variety of other designations. However, what Tom taught me went way beyond anything I had ever heard of. The second book "we" wrote encompassed what he taught me about healing: Tom: Cosmic Healing. Apparently, there are more books to come about different kinds of healing. I am excited about it but have no idea yet, what it is about.

This is the third book and it is about the lessons Tom is learning and teaching me along the way. It also includes his continuing experiences with other people.

When Tom first told me to write this book, I was apprehensive. In my mind, there was one very strong message that Tom taught me from the other side, and I believed people needed to know: as long as we engage in the lessons on this side, we can easily resolve or complete it/them on the other side; we don't need to complete the lessons on this side!!! We just have to engage!

That was a huge lesson for me. It took a huge load off of me because I am always working at embracing my "higher potential". Now I just have to engage as opposed to complete – that's pretty big, at least for me.

But what were the other lessons he wanted to convey? I had no idea. But once again, all I had to do was trust him. This book was completed in a couple of days, in between seeing clients, writing reports, and working on the new house; and there was certainly more than one lesson!

In my mind, I wrote it as he directed it. But when I "finished" the next morning he told me we had a lot of work left to do. I was supposed to re-arrange all the chapters, which meant editing the flow of the book. And I was supposed to add a few more things in. Personally, I thought that was funny. I asked why he didn't organize it the way he now wanted, in the first place. He claimed that it was because **he** didn't know how it was going to unfold. He was given help and direction with his guides as he or we went along. Oh well. As usual, I can neither argue or prove these things, I can only share them with you and let you decide what you want with to do with them.

Throughout the book, I have copied and pasted several of the conversations with Tom. His responses are always in italics. In addition, I have also copied/pasted transcriptions of what psychics/mediums/channelers have said. My books are all have the same fonts: me, my conversations with Tom; Tom; psychics.

I hope you enjoy the book. As always, take what resonates with you and leave the rest, maybe for another time.

Chapter 2

Relationships Across Dimensions

This was one of the first chapters I had to re-arrange because Tom decided that the chapters were in the wrong order. Initially, this chapter began entirely differently. Oh well. I don't know about you, but I think that's a hoot.

Prior to Tom crossing over, I had never thought of personally having a relationship with a soul/energy/entity, whatever you call a loved one, once they have crossed over. We had read about people that did have connections with others across the dimensions, I never thought about it happening with me or between Tom and myself. But that didn't stop it from happening.

From the first day Tom crossed over, I could "feel" him hug me during the day and cuddle me in the night. Yet again, it never occurred to me, at that point, that we would be able to establish any kind of relationship, across the dimensions.

During those early days I had an unbelievable drive to write poetry. Poems to, about, and for Tom. When he woke me in the night, cuddling me, the poetry would just flow through my head. Then in the morning, I had this incredible drive to write it all down before I did anything else.

I wrote over 80 poems. And as I keep saying, "I am not a poet."

The poetry was obviously a huge part of my grieving process, but the poems also provoked thoughts and questions about whether I was using the poetry to stay connected with Tom; as well as, could I stay connected with Tom; and of course, should I stay connected with Tom. As I wrote the poems, there were more and more poems asking Tom to stay with me. I was in conflict, I did not want to get in his way of healing, growing or learning or doing whatever he was doing on the other side, but I wanted to stay connected with him. So, I simply asked if he could share his journey with me.

One of the poems I wrote, conveyed the conflict well.

I Don't Want to Push You

Good morning My Love
How are you today
I want to believe you are doing okay
But I don't want to push you

I want to know what you're doing on the other side
I really don't want you to hide
I need to believe that you are enjoying the ride
But I don't want to push you

I hope it is all you thought it would be

I hope you are enjoying the journey
And I wish you would share it all with me
But I don't want to push you

You probably know by now
How much I loved you then & now
Long before a couple we allowed
But I tried not to push you

I was in love with you
And wanted a couple to be
But I didn't know how you felt about me
I didn't want to push you

I waited for you to make the move
I wanted so much for us to grove
I didn't know if us you would approve
I didn't want to push you

When you decided a couple, we became
My heart was thrilled that you felt the same
Yet how I felt I could not name
I didn't want to push you

I wanted so much to tell you I loved you
But I didn't want you to feel pressured too
Or feel that you were cornered that's true
I didn't want to push you

You massaged so well
In your hands I was jell
You made my mind a wishing well
But I didn't want to push you

Then you began to pleasure me more
I had no idea what was in store
I just knew I kept wanting more and more
But I didn't want to push you

Each step of the way, you opened my heart more
It was scary for me to keep wanting more
I had no idea what was in store
But I didn't want to push you

Friends said I should confront you
But I was so afraid, that to do
I was afraid I might lose you
I didn't want to push you

But at each step of the way
You would make my day
I learned I could count on you
To make everything okay
So I learned not push you

So now I'm in the same place
I don't want to fall from your grace
But I think there would be no better place
Than to still be with you

So, I keep telling you just what I want
That your healing & learning takes precedence
But you must know I still want your presence
But I still don't want to push you

I believe I have to be more honest now
Without worrying about you somehow
You can probably read my mind anyhow

So, you know I don't want to push you

And you also have to know
That you can always say no
I have tried to teach you that it is so
And so I don't want to push you

I love you and want the best for you
I am just hoping that includes me too
But the bottom line is
I don't want to push you

When I wrote the poem, I really had no idea what I was asking for, other than to somehow stay connected with Tom. Could he share his journey with me? If so, how? Would I see it, feel it, hear about it – no idea. How would we connect? Through meditation or automatic writing, or visualizations – again I had no idea.

As we moved along, one friend that I shared what was going on with, was concerned about me. When she heard how I was questioning myself about the new emerging connection with Tom and how it was continuing and expanding, and not diminishing, she suggested that I go to a psychic. She even did some research to find one that had a good reputation and made me a list with names and contacts. Some friends are just terrific.

I thought that might be a good idea and decided to go back to Jane. As I mentioned previously, Tom and I had a session with Jane way back when, we were just friends. She provided a lot of really detailed information although much more about Tom than me. So, I made an appointment with her. I liked going to Jane, because she did sessions over the phone which meant she couldn't physically read any facial expressions or body behavior. I could also email the questions in advance, so that she couldn't read my tone.

This second session ended with Jane saying,

- *The two of you had a very strong love and you helped him heal a lot*

Then later in the session:

- *The love between you is still very much there and is still strong*

- *Your relationship is very much alive and will continue*

It would continue? I sat in prayer or meditation or maybe you would just call it silence, for a long time after that call. What did that mean. How would it unfold. I felt Tom's arms around me and as usual that was comforting. But was he telling me that was the relationship? That I would just forever *"feel"* him put his arms around me. I loved the feeling of his hugs and yes it was comforting, but was that what Jane meant by *"Your relationship is very much alive and will continue"?*

As I mentioned earlier, about a week later, another friend phoned up and told me about a psychic/medium friend, Mary, that she knew. This woman had been a medium since she was a young child; her parents and her grandparents were also psychic. And, she had been trained by several masters.

Okay, that sounded interesting. I phoned and made the appointment with Mary. The session lasted for a few hours and she never even charged anything. She claimed that the work "she did" helped strengthen the relationships between us here and those on the other side. Well that sounded good. At the end of the session she said,

- *He keeps saying how much he loves you and he is there with you*
- *The more you believe and trust in him, the stronger your relationship will get*

I had to laugh. Believe and trust in Tom? That wasn't the problem. Believing and trusting in me was the issue.

After this session with Mary, Suzanna and I went to the "Messages from the Other Side" program, that I mentioned earlier.

I already explained that the first medium came up to me and I nodded my head, yes, when she asked if she could talk with me. They told me that my mother had recently crossed over and was sending lots of love and healing to both me and my Dad. They talked about Tom and addressed the questions I had asked Tom to address from the previous day; and congratulated me on selling the house – which I had sold four hours before!!!

At the end of the "reading", Terry, said,

- *"Your husband wants you to write a book*
- *Again, he really does love you; it's important to understand how much he loves you*
- *You will continue to develop your relationship but not all at once."*

The following week, Suzanna and I went to a meditation group that ended with Donna, a Channeler, who answered questions for anyone in the room. After everyone else's questions, Donna asked, "Is Holly here?"

I was at the back of the room and raised my hand saying, "Yes, I'm here."

Donna said,

- *Tom is here. He has been here all night.*
- *This is what I got from him:*
    - *She is my bright light*
    - *She is my true love*
    - *She is my helper*

Further along she said,

- *He actually wants to stay with you*
- *He knows you love him enough to let him go*
- *He loves you and wants to be with you during this time*

After some other comments she said,

- *Actually, you are inseparable*

- *You come from the same soul group*
- *You will journey together*
- *You will never be apart*
- *You made an agreement, made on the other side for the purpose of creating more love*
- *To fulfill each others' shoes*
- *To allow each other to learn and expand at your soul level*

She deviated but came back and continued on,

- *Your relationship will develop in increments*
- *You will always be able to feel his presence*
- *But you cannot stay in the same place – continue to move forward*

Wow! Okay, so we have four out of four saying we will continue to develop a relationship. They obviously believed that relationships could occur across dimensions. The challenge was, I had never talked with anyone on the other side. But around that time, the following poem emerged from me.

I use the term emerged, because I never sat down and thought about writing poetry. The drive to write was like an addiction that I wasn't in control of. When I wrote, it just flowed. I didn't have to think about what I wanted to write, it just flowed out of me. I would go back and read what I had written with amazement. Wow! I just wrote that? Tom has more to say about that in another chapter.

What If….

What if…this was meant to be
What if…we agreed to this before we came to be

What if…we agreed that we would connect again
What if…we agreed that we would become friends

Supposedly we've already been parent and child
Supposedly we had a great marriage upon which God smiled

What if…we had already agreed
That in this life you would choose me to leave

What if …we agreed that you would go to the other side
What if … we agreed that we needed to be on either side

What if…we agreed that we wanted to learn to connect
What if…we agreed to communicate across the big disconnect

What if…we agreed that a friendship we would create
What if…we agreed that from that love we would take

What if…we believed that connection we could make
What if…we believed that our love this could take

What if…we believed you and me
Could take this challenge and make it be

The ultimate love that could connect across time
A love that across the dimensions could climb

I have learned to believe in you and me

I believe in what you wanted to be

I believe that all this could be true
So, I am waiting and open just for you
I believe that you can make it all come true

Thank you for connecting like you have
But I believe we can do more than that

I await your direction
As we make this injection
To our understanding of the connection

It will be built on our reflections
Just give me direction
You have all my affection...Love and more

Several months later, Tom and I had the following discussion. By the time this conversation took place, we had established the ability for one-hour conversations, which we engaged in every morning. Remember, when Tom and I are conversing the text is in italics.

(Me) Why am I crying?

(Tom) Maybe because you just wish I was loving you on that side. Or maybe it is because when you feel so full of love you just have to release it somehow and you do that with tears. I can feel your love and I feel how immense it is for you. You have such a huge heart. I think that is why you can work with the emotional portals. Your emotion is so incredibly deep.

I wonder if that is why you sometimes scared me on the other side...I had never felt that kind of love before. Yet, I always knew we had something deep and special. I guess it always comes back to I just didn't feel good enough.

You operated at such a high level and I just didn't believe I could. You saw through the behaviours and the crap and the fears and the programs and you saw the real me...I wish I could have embraced that more when I was over there. We were supposed to go further than we did before I crossed over. But ultimately this is what we are supposed to be doing. We just started earlier than we had previously agreed to.

Hold on a minute, you can see or know what our souls agreed to before we came into this life?

Yes, I am aware of what we agreed to and I am now also aware of what we did previously to get here.

Holy S**t, why didn't you tell me!?! Can you elaborate?

I don't know. I know we agreed to get together again, and I know that we agreed to become partners again and I know that we agreed to continue our relationship in this way. You know that poem you wrote, <u>What If</u>...that was huge for me. It helped me to see what we were meant to do.

I think that was your Higher Self coming through and telling you to keep going, not to give into the grieving, keep reaching out to me because it was dead on...ha ha 'pardon the pun' as you would say.

You had a lot of help in those first few weeks, there were a lot of guides helping you pull through. A lot of the poetry you wrote was coming through others, that is why you were so driven. Your guides and various other helpers were all there helping you, including your Mom.

And then of course, there was me. Helping you move through your stuff, helped me...and how you dealt with it all helped me...we were a team even then. That seems like so long ago.

As I mentioned, at the time of writing this third book, I spent at least an hour every day talking with Tom. He connected with several people on this side, including my Dad and the general contractor for the new house. That was huge, and I will further elaborate on that in another chapter.

The challenge for me was, the psychics, mediums, channelers, whatever, were all familiar to the concept. Well actually the concept was familiar with me as well. Just not the experience. And I still had no idea what to expect. But it was comforting to know that the relationship would in some way continue.

So yes, many if not most people believe, that when people "die", and I will have more to say about that word and other words in another chapter, their energy or soul or something goes to another place. People have a number of different belief systems about the "after life". It might involve heaven or hell; or into the astral or another plane; or other dimension; or other beliefs. So, unless you are an atheist, we can all agree that when people go to the other side, they have not "died". They have simply moved across into another "dimension".

However, most of us in this Western culture have not been taught how to "establish" relationships across dimensions or if that is even possible. Well, apparently, if we are open enough to connecting with them, then we can. However, having said that, I think there may be several variables that may play into developing that new kind of relationship.

Issues that might affect establishing a "cross-dimensional" relationship

The following is a short list of a few thoughts I have had, that may or may not be important to establishing an ongoing relationship with someone who has crossed over; followed by a bit of a commentary on them:

Beliefs:

1. Do you believe that a relationship across dimensions can develop?
2. Does the one who crossed over believe that a relationship can develop across dimensions?
3. What are your other beliefs surrounding a possible relationship?
4. Are your own self doubts blocking you?
5. Would you question your own sanity if you started to feel or see or hear someone from the other side?

Emotions:

6. Are you afraid of the connection?
7. Are you afraid of what other people might think if you connect?
8. Are there other emotions going on for you that are preventing you from establishing a relationship, i.e., grieving, anger, sadness, frustration, hurt, etc.?

Purpose:

9. Does the other person have to do some of their own work first, before they can connect with you?
10. Do you need to do some of your work before you can connect with them?
11. Is there a purpose for the connection for you or for the other?

Preparation:

12. Have you both, together or individually, prepared for it while on this side?
13. Have you prepared for it in other lifetimes or in other dimensions?
14. Do you need to have any spiritual preparedness or development on this side?
15. How self aware are you: of energy inside your body; or outside of your body
16. How sensitive are you to what is going on around you on a subtler level?

Chemical issues:

17. Are pharmaceutical drugs getting in the way?
18. Are entertainment drugs getting in the way?
19. Is alcohol getting in the way?
20. Is your diet getting in the way?

So, let's explore these variables in a little more depth.

#1 Do you believe that a relationship across dimensions can develop?

I have certainly always believed that people can connect with those on the other side, but I never thought it would happen for me or attempted it in any way. Actually, I just never thought about me having a connection with someone on the other side. But I have now learned of others who didn't believe it could happen and yet have had experiences.

One example is my father. I know my father has experienced several connections with my grandfather. Papa appeared several times and had conversations with my Dad, starting about 10 years after Papa crossed over. My Dad's Mom and his sister have also appeared several times to him, although they never talk. He asks them if they want to say or ask anything, but they never do.

The point here is, my Dad was never interested in spirituality or philosophies or esoteric conversations. He never thought about it; simply accepted it when it happened.

And of course, there are those who really want it to happen, and haven't had any experience. So, this variable, in and of itself, is insufficient.

#2 Does the one who crossed over believe that a relationship can develop across dimensions?

When Tom and I explored these more esoteric conversations, they were usually about us both crossing over together and what might happen. For a long time before we became romantic, Tom referred to us as "Ascension Partners". But he definitely believed it could happen, I just don't know that he thought it would happen with us. Or for that matter, between him and others.

He certainly never shared any thoughts of that nature with me, if he did.

NOTE: by the time I was editing this book, Tom elaborated on who else he makes contact with or doesn't; who he has watched either regularly or intermittently; and why. I was very surprised. It wasn't at all what I would have thought. But then none of this process is.

#3 What are your other beliefs surrounding a possible relationship?

Tom and I both had plenty of beliefs around this type of thing. We didn't always agree. But then my Dad had no beliefs surrounding it, other than to think it was all "flaky stuff". Yet he has seen Tom and others.

#4 Are your own self doubts blocking you?

I certainly can understand that if we have self doubts, it would block the connection. On the other hand, I had months of self doubting and self-questioning, and it still continued to grow.

#5 Would you question your own sanity if you started to feel or see or hear someone from the other side?

I was a psychologist for 20 years. I certainly started to question my own sanity as the connection continued and developed. Was it my mind struggling to cope with all the grieving? Was I losing it?

Despite friends having a variety of experiences with Tom as well, I was still self questioning. As I have already said, I went to various psychics, mediums, channelers, etc. to see what they said. I was always very careful not to provide any information. I wanted to have clarity about what was coming from the other side and not influence the reading or give them any information to build on.

I researched online and went to a number of sites of professionals and scientists who had similar experiences.

Eventually, I gave up the self doubt and self questioning. And, the more I gave it up, the stronger Tom came through.

#6 Are you afraid of the connection?

I certainly wasn't afraid of any connection. I wanted it. But I know many people have commented that they couldn't handle it, if it were them. Several people have made comments along the lines of, "he better not show up to me" or "S**t that would scare the H**l out of me".

I would think fear would block most channels.

#7 Are you afraid of what other people might think if you connect?

There is another aspect to fear. You may not be afraid if someone connected with you across the dimensions, but you may be afraid of what others would say or think of you if you had those kinds of experiences.

In consideration of the fact, that this is still a fear, I would think the same blocking process would apply.

Now I strongly believe that fear isn't always a bad thing. In fact, fear has its place and can protect us. But I think if we were afraid of the connection, we would probably block it.

Yet, again, I was doubting myself and at some point, afraid of what others might think if I actually shared what was going on or wrote a book and published it, yet, the connection remained. Of course, I wasn't initially planning on writing anything. I just kept notes for myself. But repeatedly the topic came up with both Tom and the psychics, so I cautiously started to entertain the idea.

#8 Are there other emotions going on for you that are preventing you from establishing a relationship, i.e., grieving, anger, sadness, frustration, hurt, etc.?

What about other emotions? Perhaps any strong emotion may block the connection. Which may be why psychics etc. can have better connection than the person at hand. The psychics don't have any emotional ties to either party.

There may be elements of the grieving process, whether it be anger or sadness or hurt or any other emotion, that may get in the way.

Another emotion that might get in the way is wanting it too much rather than allowing it. I was told repeatedly, not to push "seeing" Tom. I needed to let go of the "desire" and simply "allow". From my perspective, that is a difficult one. When you really want something, how do you simply "let go" and "allow". That was a big lesson for me.

#9 Does the other person have to do some of their own work first, before they can connect with you?

I think it is rather narrow of us to assume that the other party should simply be able to connect. Do they have their own healing, learning, growing to do? For instance, I asked Tom why my Mom wasn't connecting with me or my Dad (and considering I had Tom, I really pushed for my Mom to connect with my Dad). Tom explained that she her journey was different from his and currently she was in a "healing process".

He didn't have a lot of connection with my Mom. But depending on what Tom and I were working on, she sometimes appeared.

As a side note, when my Mom comes around, it is like she "flits" in and out very quickly, which makes sense. My Mom always did everything very fast. BUT, her energy is really glittery which wasn't my Mom at all. She thought glittery things were for young children. So why is her energy glittery? No idea.

To continue with the side note, when I came back to edit this book months after I had written it, I had had a recent session with Terry who said:

- *Your Mom is coming through – not Tom – coming through in a very relaxed fashion. She usually has an excitement about her...*

Interesting, we had never before discussed Mom's energy and usually it was Tom that was dominant. Apparently, Mom was helping me with something which I was struggling with. But the fact that Terry said her energy usually had an excitement about it, seemed to validate my experience of her.

Moving back to Tom, he attempted to help the connection between my parents. The first time my Dad saw my Mom, Dad immediately phoned me up and asked me, to ask Tom, if that was really her. Dad was self doubting, and again like me, it was because he wanted it so bad. So, he was questioning whether it was really Mom or was his mind creating it. "Like father, like daughter?" Or perhaps that might be the same for a lot of people. Anyways, by this time, he had experienced Tom and had faith in Tom and talked with Tom frequently, although his conversations were one sided.

Tom was able to provide answers for my Dad through me and we continue to hope, eventually through Dad directly. Another time, my Dad heard my Mom. He thought she sounded angry or frustrated with him. He didn't know what he had done wrong. So again, he phoned me and asked me to ask Tom.

Tom explained that Dad didn't do anything wrong, but rather, Mom had been trying to get his attention and she was frustrated. He heard the frustration in her voice. Interesting.

#10 Do you need to do some of your work before you can connect with them?

Another possible variable might be whether there is any purpose for the connection. Certainly, with Tom and I, I have been told repeatedly, by Tom and others, that there is a purpose. On the other hand, we don't know what purpose there is with my grandparents and my aunt showing up to my Dad.

I could get really ego-centric and suggest that it prepared my Dad so that he could be the great support he now is for me? But I really have no idea.

#11 Is there a purpose for the connection for you or for the other?

Do we need to prepare for the connection on this side? Certainly, Tom and I did a lot of things that could be considered esoteric. Again, Tom claims that we not only prepared for all this on this side, with the things that we were conscious of, but we also prepared at levels we were not even aware of. Well, I can't argue that. I have no idea. But consciously, we never did anything with the intent of developing a relationship across dimensions.

It does, however, bring into question, how many things are we actually doing, perhaps at different levels of consciousness, that we have no idea of in our simplistic three-dimensional minds – that we like to think of as reality?

Again, we can also look at my Dad's experiences. I have spent a lifetime exploring religions, spirituality and esoteric concepts, so the theory might apply to me. But my Dad is the exact opposite, he used to think that this was all just "flaky stuff" and wasn't interested.

It was 'woo woo' or 'flaky' until he had his first experience with Papa.

So, do we need to prepare for it on this side? It doesn't appear to be the case.

#12 Have you both, together or individually, prepared for it while on this side?

While, I am having a big enough challenge being aware of what we might have done in this lifetime preparing for the work, I certainly have no recall of other lifetimes or other dimensions. Yet Tom claims that we have worked on this in other life times. All I can say is "Okay, if you say so."

#13 Have you prepared for it in other lifetimes or in other dimensions?

What about when it comes to being spiritually developed? I would like to think that I am a spiritual person. I have certainly spent a life time working with spirituality and strongly believe that religiosity is very different from spirituality.

Certainly, Tom was a very spiritual person as well. He was definitely not religious.

But again, my Dad? I don't think so. He just wasn't interested. On the other hand, he was a very moral, honorable man and some people think that the two go hand in hand, regardless of what your beliefs are.

#14 Do you need to have any spiritual preparedness or development on this side?

How aware do you need to be? Well again, I can see energy around people and plants; I can also see the plasma in the atmosphere; so perhaps you could say I have more awareness. But on the other hand, my Dad doesn't; whereas Tom was learning to see energies.

#15 How self aware are you: of energy inside your body; or outside of your body

I have a good awareness of my body's energy and certainly, a lot more so now than before. I can feel energy flow in the acupuncture meridians.

Now I can feel energetic shifts, although I have no vocabulary to describe them, when I am working with Tom.

Tom was always able to feel or sense my acupuncture meridians even though he had no training whatsoever.

But my Dad can't.

I am also aware of differences in energies in a room. But once again, my Dad had no awareness of those types of energies at all. Further, I have met people who do have that kind of awareness but have no connection across dimensions.

#16 How sensitive are you to what is going on around you on a subtler level?

Some people are very aware of different types of psychodynamics and energetic exchanges between people; while others are not.

But while I am aware of people who have different levels of perception, I have no awareness of how that variable correlates with connecting across dimensions.

#17 Are pharmaceutical drugs getting in the way?

I would think that pharmaceutical drugs would block any perceptions of more subtle energies. They are toxic to the body; cause nutrient depletion; and a host of other issues. But I have never seen any studies or have any awareness of how they correlate with connecting across dimensions.

On the other hand, they may cause illusions and delusions.

#18 Are entertainment drugs getting in the way?

This may be a more confusing variable. Many claim, that various herbal/plant concoctions are used in rituals to create a connection or eliminate the blockages that prevent connections.

Others will claim that what the compounds are doing is creating a serotonin or other toxicity that is misunderstood. I am not in a position to argue this point, as I have never taken or researched entertainment drugs or mushrooms or anything of the kind.

#19 Is alcohol getting in the way?

Again, I have never drank alcohol. However, I can imagine how the chemical toxicity from alcohol could either create delusions or block any real experience.

#20 Is your diet getting in the way?

The belief in Ayurveda medicine, is that meat products block or prevent spiritual advancement.

In our culture, I would think that the toxins in foods and the processed or microwaved or GMO or fast food would cause blockages as they are toxic to the body.

Bottom line is – I don't have a clue. It would seem that I have done a lot to believe, prepare, focus and be aware, as did Tom. But my Dad did none of it and he has had some interesting experiences. Obviously, the reason I repeatedly use my Dad as an example, is because we are total opposites.

I could suggest, that it has more to do with levels that we are not aware of. But again, it is only a suggestion, as I have no awareness of those other levels that are often discussed in more esoteric readings.

What dies a relationship across dimensions look like?

If, however, we can get past how or why we can establish a relationship across different dimensions, then we might want to look at what a relationship like that might look like?

I would imagine, just like every relationship on this side is different, so is every relationship across dimensions.

How you communicate is a good place to start. Psychics claim there are many different types of "claires". "Claire" means "clear" but is used to refer to the different methods we connect with other energies. The four main ones are:

Clairaudience: **Hearing**. This is the one I think I do best now. I can hear fairly easily, especially when I am sitting, concentrating in front of the computer. This is probably correlated with both the amount of time I have spent there transcribing our conversations as well as my focus when there, transcribing. Clairaudient is difficult to explain because it is not hearing outside your head with your ears, but it is not hearing inside your head like when you are talking with yourself. It is very different than both. I have attempted to create it in several ways without success.

Clairvoyance: **Seeing**. Clairvoyance is about seeing. I work at being able to "see" Tom. It comes and goes but usually without my intent – I am working at achieving the capacity, 'with intent'. For some reason, it is really important to me, but as mentioned earlier, I am told that as long as I really "want" it, it will evade me. Not fair. But then who ever said life was fair?

Clairsentience: **Feeling**. Clairsentience is the ability to receive messages through feelings, emotions, or physical sensations. I have only experienced the emotional component of this a few times. It is pretty powerful when it happens. I have a friend who works a lot with this one now, thanks to Tom, and it can leave her really wiped out or really energize her.

I say, now, because prior to Tom and I connecting, she had no connection with ones who had crossed over. But now because of Tom, she now connects with four people on a regular basis: her father (who crossed over, over 40 years ago); her husband (who crossed over 11 years ago); her husband's mother and her mother, once; and both her grandmothers – although one is a lot more prevalent than the other.

On the other hand, right from the beginning, I could "feel" Tom's energy. I could feel him put his arms around me during the day; feel him cuddle me at night; then eventually feel him kiss me, tickle me, etc.

Clair cognizance: **Knowing**. I think this one is more like what we call intuition. For instance, the morning my Mom crossed over, I told my Dad that she was going today. He asked me how I knew. I explained that I had no idea how I knew, I just knew she was going today. And she did.

However, I think there are many times that when we call "it" intuitive, it is just our brains/mind putting together information and associations. So, we need to learn to differentiate. But how?

It would be nice if we just knew how to separate out what the mind can do through association on a subconscious level, from what is truly intuition, from what is coming through due to those on the other side. Because I didn't initially know how to separate this out, I did a lot of self questioning and researching.

So, if we can communicate does that mean we have a relationship? In my mind, I think a relationship involves development of some kind.

Certainly, when we think of relationships on this side, it has to develop. If the relationship doesn't develop, or if we don't put effort and energy into it, it will become stagnant or bankrupt.

I would think the same occurs across dimensions. If we put effort into the relationship, it will develop and continue. On the other hand, that doesn't mean we have to be in love with the person. I would think the level of emotional connection, cognitive connection or spiritual connection that you have with the other, might be reflective of the purpose of the connection; how much time you have spent together in this lifetime and across lifetimes or dimensions.

There are probably all kinds of variables that we don't even know about and consequently, don't know what or how to ask. And of course, there are probably a multitude of people who know far more about what and how to ask, than I.

So, if I acknowledge that I am coming from a place of ignorance, then let's look at the relationship between Tom and I and see if we can figure anything out. It is funny, Tom just says, *"Well just use us as an example."*

#1) Tom and I acknowledged that we had a very deep love as friends

#2) Then we acknowledged that the love between us as partners seemed to have a difference

#3) One could say, Tom and I spent a lot of time preparing for this in ways we were conscious of, as well as, although without conscious intent, ways we weren't conscious of.

#4) When Tom crossed over, there was a lot of emotion but there was also the clairsentience, I could "feel" him hug me right away

#5) As much as there was a lot of self doubt and self questioning there was also an openness and desire for the connection

#6) Once the different types of validation and confirmation were established, our ability for clairaudience developed

#7) While I have seen Tom numerous times, it is usually "without intent". It still comes and goes without my ability to control it. So, I am still working on that.

#8) Since we have established the connection, Tom has spent an incredible number of hours teaching me a variety of things. First it was about hearing him; then seeing him; then OBEs (Out of Body Experiences); then astral travel. He has the 'patience of Job' but always pushes me to keep going. As his abilities increase on the other side, he teaches me.

So, what is the bottom line? We are both open to and working with the connection and attempting to develop the relationship.

So, can you have a relationship across dimensions. Absolutely. How? Why? I don't really know.

I do know, that I thought Tom was an awesome individual on this side, but he is proving to be even more so on that side. And yes, relationships can and do continue across the dimensions. A huge lesson for me.

Chapter 3

What is a Soul Mate?

One question I didn't ask or address in the chapter on relationships across dimensions, was whether you need to be soul mates to have that kind of relationship.

What are soul mates? Are they the ones that you live happily ever after with? Are they the ones that provoke you to learn or engage in your lessons? Are they the ones that travel across time with you? Are they part of the same "soul group" as you? And if so, what is a soul group or how is it formed? Are they the ones that you have agreed to work with? Ultimately, I don't know. I have been given a variety of answers.

As mentioned previously, Donna said,

- *He actually wants to stay with you*
- *He knows you love him enough to let him go*
- *He loves you and wants to be with you during this time*
- *Actually, you are inseparable*
- *You come from the same soul group*
- *You will journey together*
- *You will never be apart*

- *You made an agreement, made on the other side for the purpose of creating more love*
    - *To fulfill each others' shoes*
    - *To allow each other to learn and expand at your soul level"*

Terry's take on it was,

- *Tom – he is not a guide – he is a soul mate*
- *He travels with you*
- *You have been in prior lives before*
- *Your purpose is very intertwined*
- *He wants you to do automatic writing*
- *You can start with pen and paper and then move into typing – no you are a good typist – you can start with the typing – he is impatient for you to start – wants you to write his book*
- *You are not in the right space right now – you will be shortly – practice now, right away*
- *Tom is impatient*
- *You share the same vision*

Jane, the second psychic I saw, said,

- *Your husband crossed over recently, he is your soul mate not your guide*

Tom has talked about it several times...

I know you asked about the differences between twin souls, soul mates, soul group, and I saw you research it. I'm not sure I can explain it to you. The terms people use are inaccurate and fuzzy. Just know that we are together, and our love will guide us.

So, I heard you ask in your head – so how does that impact on our love. Is it simply because we are intertwined or are we so intertwined because of our love? It comes to me that it is both and even more. We are so intertwined because of our love and our mutual agendas and purpose. We have a profound love because we know how to love each other with a general universal love and care for one another, as we do for everyone; but also because of the love we have developed as friends; and also because of the romantic love we have shared, and we have done this in many lifetimes. And don't forget the parental/child love that we have also shared. In all of our lifetimes we are able to further develop our love for one another over there. But we also do that in other lifetimes and in other dimensions.

And because we are soul mates. And because we are from the same soul group. This just keeps coming to me. There is so much. We also share a wonderful laughter. It seems to be another thread that weaves throughout all the lifetimes. I hope you understand that I am learning or remembering all of this as we are talking this morning. I wasn't aware of all of this before. Well some of it, but there always seems to be more. That sounds like something you would say.

I had always teased Tom during the 6 months between our birthdays, that he was an 'old man'. So, when he was on the other side, I attempted to tease him as well…

I was just thinking on this side you would be 58 today but how old are you on that side?

There is no beginning and no end and no time so there is no age.

So, I can call you an 'old fart' then? Remember, on this side, you are now an 'old man' for the next 6 months!

But I'm not on that side - so it doesn't count.

But on that side, you are even older!!

But on this side, we are the same age – we are soul mates that have been together forever.

Guides

Once Terry introduced me to my "guides", I wanted to know how that would impact on us…

Now that I am working with the guides, will that affect how we work?

Yes, it will, I hope. It will enhance it. I am a soul mate and not a guide. I have my guides and you have yours and we have a few between us. They will all help us achieve what we are supposed to do together.

About a month later, I was frustrated when I explained to Terry I didn't always know when it was Tom, me or us. She said that was because Tom and I are so intertwined. I didn't like that. I wanted boundaries and to know when it was or wasn't me.

Remember when you asked Terry if it was me or you that you were hearing…she said it was both…that we were very intertwined…I think that is what she meant…our thoughts affect one another across the veil…I have noticed that a few times but didn't stop to work it out – just had this vague awareness. Putting it into words or maybe even just attending to it more, helps me understand what I was aware of but wasn't clear about.

Okay, sounds good but I don't know if I am comfortable with that. How do I know when thoughts are mine or are yours or are ours? Maybe this is my ego, or I am being possessive or something, but I would like to have clarity.

Yeah, I saw that reaction...interesting...you know when it is me or you, but when it is us...I think that is more about we each just have impact on the other. Maybe this goes on for most people with their guides or higher self and they are just not aware of it ... like you used to suggest...that's the basis of intuition...

Okay that makes sense, and of course, I like it because it agrees with one of my theories...ha ha...but you are not a guide or my higher self...we are separate...I think somewhere along the line, we were told that we were soul mates and part of the same soul group – do you agree?

Yes, but we are also very intertwined at a very deep level. I think it goes deeper than most that have this kind of connection. As you would say, and there are probably those that go a lot deeper...I am just suggesting that we go deeper than most...

The concept came up again a few weeks later,

This may seem like a weird question, but when we are both on that side, who is the guiding force? I really don't care who, but I am curious.

Well I don't think either of us. I think when we are both here...we work with our guides, the angels, the ascended masters, whoever is available to help us grow and learn on this side.

Do we grow and learn together or separately? I have never thought of this stuff before, so I appreciate you being patient and answering my questions.

Because we are intertwined, soul mates in the same soul group working with the same intention and purpose, I think we do both. We would each have our own path at one level but at another level we would work together.

In the same way that our higher levels of DNA move in and out in a quantum manner constantly affecting all the other levels, I think we move in and out and affect one another on some levels.

So, what is a soul mate? I think that maybe soul mates may come from the same soul group. I think it is apparent that they are not each other's guides. And there may be a cross over regarding whether they travel through lifetimes and/or dimensions together and whether they have a joint agenda.

Another consideration involves something else Terry said,

- *You two have a very deep connection*
- *You are the only one who can do this*
- *Even the angels – say that you are the right person for this process*
- *He believes in angels*
- *He accepts a lot more than before*

Does being soul mates have something to do with the angels? I will let you play with that one on your own.

I don't think soul mates need to be antagonistic to push one another to address issues and grow and learn and heal. I think they can be friends or romantic partners in different lifetimes. Tom and I have also, apparently, been parent and child, and best friends in different lifetimes.

So maybe the underlying characteristic, is that they have a deep love for one another; have a similar or entwined agenda; and travel through lifetimes together.

I like simple and that makes it simple.

Chapter 4

Forgiveness

One of my girlfriends, Katherine, was awesome during those first few weeks after Tom crossed over. During the first few days, she phoned every hour on the hour to make sure I was okay. Then gradually weened down to once a day. Some friends are just phenomenal!!

Katherine was the one that was concerned about me questioning myself regarding whether the contact with Tom was real and suggested I go see a psychic. Interesting as she also thought this stuff was pretty "woo woo" or "flaky". Since that time, things have changed.

Earlier, I explained that Tom and I had gone to psychics at different times both together and individually. Jane had a good reputation and lived in another city, so the session was over the phone. When we phoned the first time, as friends, we only asked two questions:

1. Had we been together in prior lifetimes?
2. What was the purpose of our connection in this lifetime?

As noted earlier, she provided us with a huge amount of information during that session, although most of it was about Tom.

Mary, the second psychic who was suggested by another friend, spent three hours with me and didn't even charge me for her time!

Both of them gave me information that was validating. In a variety of ways, they confirmed that my experiences were quite real, but they also left me very concerned.

First, Tom kept saying he was so sorry he left me. Second, I was wondering why everyone kept reinforcing how much he loved me. I thought I knew that he loved me, he certainly told me he loved me, he was incredibly loving and affectionate, why was it such an important issue to "everyone".

Jane said,

- *He keeps saying "I am so sorry" and "I love you"*
- *He's like a big teddy bear – full of love*
- *He wants you to know how sorry he is – he keeps saying he loves you and that he is so sorry*

Later, she said,

- *He knows how hard you tried, and he loves you too and again he is so sorry; he keeps saying that*

When I saw the second psychic, Mary, she said,

- *He's very upset at leaving you*

- *He loved you very much*

Further on, she said.

- *Again, he's very upset*
- *He can't give you all that he wants to*
- *He's very upset, he's so sorry*
- *It will take him some time, but you will receive what he can give you*

I shared my concerns, about Tom constantly saying he was so sorry, to another terrific friend, Suzanna. She suggested that I needed to forgive him.

As I explained in the first book, this didn't fit for me. In my mind, forgiveness was between you and God, or your Higher Self, or whatever you believed in. A vertical process.

Between people, we needed to "accept" one another, our choices, and the fact that we each had our own pathway. Acceptance between people, I saw as a horizontal process.

We may not like how someone else behaves or treats us, but it is up to us what we chose to do with it. Tom knew that I thought of forgiveness as a vertical process and acceptance as a horizontal process, and he agreed with me when I explained it to him. So why would he need me to "forgive" him? I accepted that he had crossed over; and that he chose to keep going; that it was his choice. Suzanna thought maybe it had to with the fact that he chose to keep going.

I was told by different psychics that when he crossed over, he was given a choice. He could come back or keep going. It was simply a choice. There was no judgement about it.

He was told that if he kept going, he would be able to embrace his purpose in life, and that he wouldn't be able to do that if he came back. He was also told that his purpose was to work through me or with me and that our relationship would continue to grow.

So, let's put that in context. Many times, over the years, Tom and I explored how he felt like he had a purpose but didn't know how to connect with it. It felt so elusive for him. We went through a variety of exercises and even attended workshops attempting to help him identify his purpose, but he never felt like he got there.

In addition, Tom was always afraid that he would lose me. First as a friend, and then as a romantic partner and friend. We will get into that more later, but when he crossed over, apparently, he was given the opportunity to fulfill his purpose and continue with me. It seemed like a logical thing to keep going. But now he was so sorry he caused me such grief.

From my perspective, if I was in "his shoes" so to speak, I probably would have made the same choice. Tom was going to be able to fulfill his purpose; we were going to continue to develop our relationship; and we were going to be able to work together; and as a side bonus, he got to leave all his stressors behind – that was huge! At that point, he had a plateful of heavy-duty stressors. I had to agree, logically it was a good choice.

But maybe he needed to hear from me that I "forgave" him for leaving me?

I followed Suzanna's suggestion and did two major meditations on forgiveness with Tom, using the Ho'oponopono (I'm sorry. Please forgive me. Thank you. I love you.). We focused on forgiving each other for any hurt that we may have caused one another, with or without awareness. We also focused on his choosing to "keep going" when he crossed over.

The next time, I saw a medium or a psychic, was with Suzanna. That was the program called "Messages from the Other Side" that I explained earlier.

They really focused on how much "he *really* loves you" as opposed to being so focused on "he keeps saying how *sorry* he is":

Your husband is coming in strong;

...he really loves you

And later,

like he really loves you

and then again,

he really loves you a lot

and again,

Again, he really does love you

it's important to understand how much he loves you

and yes again,

He keeps sending you so much love

You need to know how much he loved you

Again, I believed that "forgiveness" is a vertical process and "acceptance" is a horizontal process. However, one should never assume various things:

- Tom needed to hear that I forgave him for making the choice he did
- Tom needed to know that I understood and accepted his decision without judgement
- We needed to acknowledge various other issues and let them go, in order to move on
- Tom needed to know that I didn't hold anything against him
- Tom needed to know that I was okay with the grieving and understood that it is just an emotion that I had to experience and work with
- Or so many other possibilities.

I never did ask him what it was that changed for him, I was just so thankful that he didn't need to focus on being sorry anymore. So, you chose.

Chapter 5

There is No Judgement

One morning, Tom said,

You know, I have never said anything about all the poems you wrote when I crossed over. They were fantastic. I was really impressed. But I think my favourite one was "What If...". I was so pleased, thankful, I'm not sure what I was, but I loved it. But there was another one, about no judgement..."

This one?

On the other side - There is no judgement

On the other side
I would like to believe there is no judgement
We can just see what we did
And accept any misjudgements

On the other side
I would like to believe we are just love
Vibrations of light that emanate from God above
We are one in the spirit, we are one in love

On the other side
I would like to believe you are free
Free from hurt and stress and pain
There is no stain, you are simply free

On the other side
I hope you hold no guilt or shame
I pray that you are born again
I want you to experience absolutely no blame

On the other side
I would like to believe we learn more easily
From the choices that we made here hazily
And I want you to do so ever so peacefully

On the other side
I would like to believe you are learning how awesome you are
How many times have I told you what a terrific man you are
That you understand that in this life you were a star

On the other side
I hope you get to experience an awesome ride
Through an awesome spiritual journey of vibration & light
An experience way to expansive for our small minds to abide

On the other side
I wish for you everything you have ever wanted it to be
A ride through the unimaginable beauty of the universe
A multi dimensional journey beyond anything I could see

On the other side
Wishing you abundance untold
I still hope you will connect with me
I want you to share with me & be bold

On the other side

I hold you in love
I hold you in beauty
Like a pure white dove

Be the love that you are...

Yup, that's the one. Those poems really helped me to move along. They helped me to connect to you. Or stay connected with you. Thank you.

It's interesting, I had never thought of it before, but forgiveness and lack of judgement are really intertwined. If there is no judgement, then there is no need to forgive. I didn't see a need for judgement and therefore, from my perspective, there was no need to forgive. I still think forgiveness has more to do with a vertical process as explained earlier, but maybe Tom needed the horizontal aspect of it acknowledged.

Like a lot of people, Tom had spent a lifetime in deprecating self-judgement. It started with his father and then continued throughout his marriage. From the time he left the marriage, he struggled with letting go of the negative self judgements.

Tom held himself in judgement for causing my self and others the pain of grieving. Recognizing that there was no judgement coming from me perhaps helped him to allow himself to let go of it. Maybe others were doing the same thing and also helping him along.

Chapter 6

Purpose

The psychic Terry said,

- *You two have a very deep connection*
- *You are the only one who can do this*
- *Even the angels say that you are the right person for this process*
- *He believes in angels*
- *He accepts a lot more than before.*

The chapter on "Forgiveness" brought up another lesson: purpose. Tom had always felt that he had a purpose but just couldn't figure out what it was. Despite the exercises we played with, and the programs we went to over the years, he never felt like he connected with his purpose.

He would make comments like, "Its something that is sitting right there, I just can't see it"; or "it's like a cloud over my head, it's always there, I wish I knew what it was" or "it's like having something sitting on my shoulder but never being able to identify what it was". If you remember, when he crossed over, he was told that if he continued to go, he would be able to fulfill his life's purpose.

One of the first few times I went to see Terry, she said,

- *You will continue the journey together*
- *It will change how you operate and how you work with transcendence*
- *You two have a very solid connection*
- *Have been in other lives together*
- *You are very intertwined*
- *He has purpose now*
- *He sees and knows what his purpose is*
- *He feels strong about it*
- *You help him with his purpose*
- *You are part of his purpose*
- *Part of his purpose is to work through you*
- *He is now manifesting what he needs to manifest, and on this side, he is manifesting it through you*

When talking about what his purpose was, Terry continued,

- *He will tell you what to write*
- *You need to follow his guidance…*
- *Tom will teach you to travel across space and time and other dimensions;*

- *He will teach you to go across different realms with intent*
- *He will teach you to open up to channeling spirit*
- *He will teach you how to access your gifts*
- *He will also teach you to see him*
- *His attention to you is particularly important because you both want to be together*
- *It is also important to both of you to help people to heal and prepare*
- *He wants you both to work it now – down the road you will have other things to do*
- *He will take you on a journey with him*

Another time she said,

- *…you will reconnect on that side – he won't reincarnate till you join him over there*
- *When you reconnect – you will have completed his life's work*

My response was, "His life's work? What about mine?"

- *Your life's work is his*
    - *You are very intertwined*
    - *Together you are enlightened…*
    - *You are more so on this side and he is more over there*
    - *Together you complete one another*

Later, she said,

- *He says: 'I had a choice and chose not to turn around'*
- *He felt he was more capable of doing things on the other side*
    - *...but he was given a choice -*
    - *He could stay here and not accomplish what he was capable of or he could go to the other side and complete the work he was meant to do with you*
- *The two of you should have melded more here...in all ways and shape and form...but he had too many fears and programs that got in the way*
- *But you will have another life together*
- *Because you are so close, you are open to do his work – which is actually your work"*

Previously, the first psychic Jane said,

- *He will wait for you on the other side and help you here and he won't come back till after you meet with him there, but it won't be for a long time yet as you still have a lot of work to do*

Later she said,

- *The two of you had a very strong love and you helped him heal a lot*
- *The love between you is still very much there and is still strong*
- *Your relationship is very much alive and will continue"*

Another theme that seemed to evolve through the different readings was that Tom would help me develop on this side...

Jane said,

- *You (Holly) are an old soul with a lot of abilities and Tom will help you develop them*

Mary said,

- *He is going to work with you from the other side*
- *He's been giving you a lot*
- *He will continue to give you whatever you need*

Terry said

- *Tom will help you with the automatic writing, but he will also help you move between dimensions with intent*
- *He will also help you to see him*
- *You will need to work at keeping balance between the different dimensions – ALL WORLDS*
- *You will work with 3-4-5th dimensions; and moving in and out of space – remember to keep it all balanced*
- *He has a lot more to offer you from the other side*
- *Tom will teach you to travel across space and time and other dimensions*
- *He will teach you to go across different realms with intent*
- *He will teach you to open up to channeling spirit*

- *He will teach you how to access your gifts*
- *He will also teach you to see him*

So, at this point we can identify two purposes: one for Tom and one for me. Apparently, for Tom to fulfill his purpose, he had to teach me to connect with him. And my purpose was apparently, to be open and receptive to connecting with him, so **we** could fulfill our purpose.

One of the many comments Tom made, in our morning conversations, was,

It is amazing to see how many of the issues we went through on that side and now with me on this side are so intertwined. We agreed to them previously. So, in a sense it makes it easier for me than for you, because I now have that awareness. So just know that. We both agreed to the processes and learning that we are doing. I have told you before how intertwined we are – it just goes very deep.

Usually we think of our life's purpose in terms of what we are meant to do on this side, but what if it is also about what we are meant to do on the other side? Maybe some of our life purpose on this side, is in preparation for the role we play or the purpose we have on the other side?

If that is the case, then that might change how people look at the process of crossing over. It becomes a whole different "ball game" if what we are doing on this side is to prepare us for a purpose on the other side. It was certainly a concept that had never occurred to me before. And of course, it provoked a lot of conversation between Tom and me.

Chapter 7

Fears Can Get in the Way

The fear I am referring to in this chapter is the fear about loving someone, not fear about connecting with someone across dimensions.

In one of the sessions I had with Terry, from "Messages from the Other Side", she told me of the underlying fears and issues Tom had about loving me. That while he told me he loved me, he had difficulty expressing how much he loved me on this side. There was a lot of fear around it.

Terry said,

- *He didn't express how much he really cared for you when here*
- *How much he really loved you*
- *He told you that he loved you, but couldn't express the depth of it, there was a lot of fear around it*

Then later she said,

- *The two of you should have melded more here...in all ways and shape and form...but he had too many fears and programs that got in the way. But you will have another life together*

Further, in one of the sessions she said,

- *Again, he says he couldn't express how much he loved you*
- *It was part of his human lesson*
- *He carried a tremendous amount of fear*
- *The fear stopped him in so many ways*

In another session, Terry said of him,

- *It involved childhood insecurities*
- *He had a huge fear of rejection – not being good enough*
- *Always had to put up a façade*

Later in the sessions, she said

- *His childhood really rendered him ineffective*
- *He has to stay aware of the lessons he learned in his childhood*
- *Most of his stuff was really deep*
- *His pain was incredibly deep*

Terry claimed that Tom said,

- *You reaching out to me and helping me, helped to realign me with my soul"*
- *I used to hide about everything*

- *I was afraid that if you understood how deep all the pain was – you would run away*
- *He says you are incredibly gentle – a lot more gentle than you think you are – you think you are hard and strong but you are not*

Later, she said,

- *Even with you – no matter how kind, encouraging, gentle and supportive you were, he was still afraid to lose you*
- *He was afraid of disappointing you*

Tom and I developed a very close relationship over the years and were able to explore a lot of issues in depth. While we were friends, we often talked about how neither of us ever wanted to be in another relationship again; how we both had our "containers of fears" that we kept safe on the shelf so that we wouldn't go into another relationship again.

We also often talked about the fears that he had of losing me, first as a friend and then both as a friend and a partner, and why. In fact, Tom learned to go pretty deep with his stuff, I was always amazed watching him go deeper and deeper with his stuff. But he really wanted to get past all of it. Especially when he started to recognize what a huge impact it had on him and how he interpreted life and thus lived his life.

The following are a few of the easier conversations with Tom:

I don't think I told you before but in some ways your love scared me. It was part of the fear. Yes, the fear was about all the crap that I had learned and experienced in my past – from my Dad, from my parents' relationship, from my ex and that was all negative.

But you scared me in a different way. You had so much to give and I was scared that I could never give you as much as you gave me. It was a 'double edge sword' as they say. I revelled in it and it gave me purpose and a new self definition but at the same time because I had huge self esteem issues and felt I wasn't good enough, it also made me feel inadequate that I could never give you the love that you gave me. As you would say, 'it was all my issue'.

I did love you to the best of my capacity, more than I had ever experienced before. It just didn't feel like it was enough. I never felt like I could do or be enough. That was a life lesson I had to deal with. You helped me so much with that. Thank you. And I love you and just know that I have far more capacity to love you from this side. And I have loved you more in other lives and in other dimensions. We have a lot of history.

Then at another time he said,

I have already been telling you how I feel for you – that I am so sorry that I couldn't express how much I loved you on that side – I could tell you I loved you – but I was so afraid of letting you know how vulnerable I was with you. You were always so much more open. You taught me a lot, but I needed to go further.

But on this side, all the fear and the programs I learned from my family and my marriage are gone. I can just tell you openly and honestly how much I love you. It is incredible and so deep and so beautiful, and I love it. I have tried to share a small amount of it with you and you got totally overwhelmed.

Don't forget that – I saw that sigh of remembrance, you had forgotten that. Don't. It is so powerful, and I am hoping when you learn to cross the dimensions with intent – that you will be able to share that with me or me with you or something.

At one point when we were discussing how emotions were different on each side, Tom said,

Well, its all good. I know how you hated it when I said that, and I am seeing you laughing. But it is all good. It means something totally different here than what I meant it on that side. Its like I am free. Free to think without being wrong...you were always good at that. You let me have my own ideas without being wrong, as opposed to my ex. When I thought of something different than her, I was just stupid.

But when I am here. There is a whole different means of thinking. I don't have to try. I don't have to worry about my thoughts. I don't get anxious with my thoughts. I get to just let them roam and they can go really wild.

Or when I think of conversations that we have had, on either side, I don't have to get concerned about whether I hurt you or not...that was always a big thing for me on that side. I was always so afraid I might hurt you and then you would leave me.

I know that is hard for you to take. You were always asking me why I would think that. But it came from childhood and from my ex. I lived with those issues my whole life, but on top of that I didn't want to hurt you, just because I loved you. I loved you so much. You have no idea.

Actually, I don't think I realized how much I loved you. It was such a scary thing for me. I know we talked about

that and you tried to help me with it, but we never went as deep as I should have gone.

If I stayed on that side, we probably would have eventually because you were always gently pushing me to go further. But here, I am just aware of it. It is enormous. I can love so much more freely now because there is no fear. No fear of you leaving; no fear of hurting of you; no fear of not being good enough; no fear of being a scumbag; no fear of you finding out I wasn't what I wanted to be; just no fear. Only love. I hope I can take a lot of this back with me when we come back together.

I don't know about you, but for me that is pretty powerful. What would life be like if we could all just come from a place of love rather than fear.

For me, it was somewhat different. I loved psychological, philosophical, esoteric conversations. I wanted to understand everything. But Tom had never discussed or thought about, a lot of the things we talked about, before.

And as much as we knew how to laugh and have fun, we also enjoyed the deeper conversations. Well, sometimes, they got a little too much for Tom and we would have to divert. But he sure learned to put out a lot.

I think it is a big lesson to learn. Not to let fear get in your way. I think a lot of people have learned or heard that it is better to come from a place of love rather than a place of fear. But regardless of how many times we have heard it, it is a good lesson to attend to.

Chapter 8

Being Good Enough

I think one of Tom's biggest fears was not being good enough. Tom knew how to put on a pretty good front. I think a lot of people believed him to be a pretty self-confident person. He knew how to hide his stuff. He had a great sense of humor and knew how to push his "crap" down.

But when you really got to know Tom, it became more and more apparent, that he had a lot of pain and anguish deep down. While he was on this side, we talked about how he had learned that he was never good enough. What could trigger those beliefs and what they did to him.

Many times, the two of us sat and cried over how human beings could be so cruel to their children or to their partners. How we each have such a capacity to hurt one another and leave lasting scars. Sometimes, they take a lifetime to heal. Sometimes, never.

We talked about how we learn to cover up our pain in life in a variety of ways and just do what we need to do. How difficult it can be to go into that kind of pain and work it through. It was kind of ironic, Tom thought that I had had a much more difficult time than he had, whereas I thought Tom had had a much more difficult time than me.

I could never understand how he could think I had a more difficult time. I grew up in a very loving home with affectionate parents. Yes, I had a very critical mother, but what he went through with his father in his young life and as a young adult was far worse.

Not believing he had any value was a major contributing factor to staying in a very abusive marriage. There were a variety of other factors that we identified over the years as well. But not believing he had any self worth or self value was huge.

I also grew up believing I was not good enough. But for entirely different reasons and I was fortunate enough in life, that I had learned how to re-write the rules many years before. But my heart went out to Tom as I saw how he struggled to rewrite the rules he had learned in life. He worked hard at both overcoming his fears and programs and at being a better person. He really was an awesome person.

As we learned to talk across the 'big divide' and worked with his guides, my guides and our guides, Tom was able to go even deeper and work through some pretty major stuff. And again, we had many discussions about how and why he learned that he wasn't good enough.

He definitely had a confidence about himself when it came to his career. He knew that he was good, he was creative, he was fast. He was confident with it.

But when it came to recognizing what an awesome individual he was, it was a whole different story. For several years on this side, we worked with different kinds of exercises, with fun and laughter, helping Tom to recognize and appreciate who he was. For the longest time, we played with an exercise where he had to tell me at least one characteristic a week, he liked, appreciated or respected about himself. Eventually he was able to come up with some ideas, but they were pretty superficial.

At one point, I got Tom to identify what he liked, appreciated or respected about me. Often times, what people like about others is what they like in themselves. That was a good exercise. It really hit home, that he was a pretty awesome man. But he had a difficult time holding onto to it. Consequently, it was difficult to allow himself to tell me how much he really loved me because it left him too vulnerable. I think that is one of the lessons that Tom came to terms with on the other side.

Love may hurt. Love makes us vulnerable. But love is also healing. When you can give and receive love in a healthy way, you can start to heal on so many levels. Truly loving the self and another and allowing another to love you, creates an incredible energy all by itself.

Love alone will not heal a personality disorder or physical issues but knowing that you are loved, allows you to start taking steps in the healing process.

At one point, Tom said,

You reaching out to me and helping me, helped to realign me with my soul.

At another point, he said,

You gave me so much. You helped me in ways I was never even aware of. You helped me to recognize things and resolve things and helped me to deal with things on so many levels. Throughout our connection, as we shifted and changed over time. You were the greatest support I ever had, and you gave so freely and without asking for anything in return.

But you can't be responsible for the lessons I came in with. You provided the pathways and the opportunities to learn. It was up to me whether I engaged in them or not. Isn't that what you always said about free choice. That our true free choice was whether we chose to engage in the lessons we came here to learn. You taught me that. And I did engage, in a lot of them. Just not all of them.

I was learning to love and trust in a way I had never done before. I learned to be open more than I ever had before. I was starting to be more aware and understand myself more than ever before. I was even trusting to talk with you about things I wouldn't have before; despite feeling like a failure; and despite all the crap that came along with it. I trusted you. And I loved you. That was huge for me.

A few months later, he said,

*And you simply **trusted** that the healing would occur. You trusted me – despite all the challenges you had with your box of fears. Despite all my issues. You had a lot more trust than I did...and you helped me develop my trust.*

Now I am helping you apply them to this work. I needed more courage and determination on that side and you helped me recognize and understand and become more aware. So now as I enhance those gifts on this side, I can be of help to you.

Repeatedly Tom claimed from the other side, and the various psychics, mediums and channelers also acknowledged, how healing our relationship and love was for Tom while he was on this side. That while he still had a long way to go, he achieved a lot of healing while he was here.

That is precious for all of us. I think many of us know that but allowing ourselves to truly come from a place of loving and honoring the self, rather than negating the self can be a challenging lesson to learn.

Repeatedly, it seemed Tom would almost get there and then he would have to connect with his ex and it wouldn't be long before he would spiral down again. Repeatedly feeling like he had to climb back up the same mountain. It was exhausting work for him and incredibly tiring. And each time, he allowed the old rules to take over, it reinforced that he just wasn't good enough.

On the other side, the lessons were huge. He was able to see who he was from my perspective; from the perspective of his higher self; and from a perspective where there was no criticism, no judgement, only love and acceptance. Recognizing that we are all on a path and that all paths eventually lead to Rome.

He was able to see through the behaviours, the coping mechanisms, the filters, the fears and the programs and simply see who he truly was. An awesome man. It was phenomenal.

What a lesson, accepting, acknowledging and appreciating who you truly are, with unconditional love and acceptance. Wow!!

Not only was he more than good enough!! More importantly, now he knew it.

Chapter 9

Engaging in the Lessons

On the one hand, many of these lessons seem very intertwined, and yet they are also all individual lessons. So yes, there was another aspect to the lessons he learned on the other side.

As long as we engage in the lessons on this side, we benefit. Our souls contract to learn various lessons when we choose to come here. Regardless of what the lessons are about, we need to engage in them.

Lessons may be about:

- Loving the self
- Trusting the self
- Respecting the self
- Honoring the self
- Forgiving the self

Or about:

- Loving others
- Trusting others with healthy boundaries
- Respecting others

- Allowing others to earn our trust
- Honoring others appropriately
- Forgiving others or accepting that their journey is theirs

Or about:

- Developing cognitively
- Establishing emotional stability
- Behaving wisely

Or about:

- Letting go of some issue
- Resolving some issue
- Learning some issue

Or about 101 other things, the point about being here, is **engaging** in the lesson. We don't need to complete the lesson or even be successful with the lesson, we simply need to engage in the lesson!!

When we choose to engage in the lesson, we can complete the work on the other side. But, if we choose to avoid, repress, deny the lessons, then we have to keep coming back until we wake up and start engaging in the lessons.

Tom worked at a number of lessons. He was always trying to be a better person. When I came back to edit this book, I had to laugh. Recently Terry had made the comment,

- *Tom says he worked really hard to be something more,*

- *It is disheartening that neither of them are doing what they could be doing, but that is their path*

She went on to explain how Tom didn't connect with people, he couldn't be of help to,

There is nothing he can do for them.

That brought up a whole bunch of questions for me that I am still working with.

Anyways, I always thought that Tom was a much more enlightened person than he gave himself credit for and one of the reasons was that he always tried so hard to be a better person. He was always wanting to better himself, even if, like most of us, not always successful. BUT, because he engaged in the lessons, he was able to resolve or complete them fairly easy once he crossed over. For me that is such a huge lesson.

Along his journey on the other side, he often told me how or what he was working with. How he went to new depths of awareness and understanding. The guides that helped him along the way. It was amazing.

For instance, one day he said,

I have full trust that you and I worked together while I was there, even on levels we weren't aware of and now while we are on different sides, we can work together even better.

At another time, he said,

Actually, we are both going at a good speed apparently. According to my Mom. She showed me a glimpse of the two of you as friends, you had a connection like you do

now with Suzanna, I think. But I am working on self definition stuff...interesting that was what you were always pushing me to work on.

I was confident in my work and in some areas of life but when it came to self value and self esteem, I handed it over to others, my Dad and my ex. You know that. We talked of that often. Well the work you started me on, I am still working on. It goes much deeper over here. But thank you for getting me going.

Then one day when I was in Terry's office she said,

- *He makes me feel good about where he is*
- *He's enlightened*
- *And it feels so right for him*
- *He will not go back to the past*

A while later she said,

- *He's letting his lessons learned, deepen*
- *He's truly embracing them at a soul level*
- *They are now a part of him and he doesn't have to go back to them again"*

I wondered what Terry meant by "he will not go back to the past". Did that mean he was going to leave me now? That he was ready to move forward? Or maybe it was something about me, that had changed that he was now going? So, I questioned Terry and she answered,

- *The past is the past for him now*
- *But you are not part of his past*
- *You are part of his present*

- *You are current with him*
- *Your work is not done because he's not finished with you yet."*

I had to laugh, "'He's not finished with me yet?' What does he mean by that?"

Terry responded,

- *There will come a time when your work is done, but it is not for a long time yet*
- *You still have 7 things or 7 projects to do together*
- *Not all of them have even started yet*
- *You will have a very long life and there is lots of work for the two of you to do.*

And then later,

- *He is now enlightened*
- *He wasn't here*
- *He knew he was missing something*
- *Always felt that there was so much missing from him*
- *He knew that you had it and he knows that absolutely now*
- *you are…very enlightened…have many gifts…*

Wow! That was huge for me. Knowing that he didn't have to come back and go through the abuse again. He had learned the lessons he came to learn. Awesome!!

Tom and I had been told before he crossed over, and various psychics have told me since he crossed over, that the abusive relationship between him and his father had been repeated across several lifetimes. So, I asked about the connection/karma with his father.

Terry replied,

- *It's all resolved*
- *Its' dealt with and gone*
- *He has brought his enlightenment up to a new notch.*

The tears rolled down my face. I was so thankful and happy for him. It was now released. He didn't have to go through it again. It was over. Wow. That was huge.

In a previous session with another medium, I asked Mary if Tom had worked through his stuff with his ex.

She replied,

- *He's not connected to her anymore*
- *He doesn't need to connect with her again on this side, but he still has learning to do.*

When I asked Terry, if his karmic lessons with his ex were resolved, she said,

- *He accepts that he once loved her, but it was never reciprocated…*
- *He gave her a piece of him*
- *He's pulling back what he gave her*

- *He gave too much trying to get a small piece back*
- *It was easier to just give, then to get back, but it left a void*
- *He's done the learning.*

Even with his ex, he had engaged in the lessons he needed to deal with here, but he finished the lessons over there. I was thrilled for him. They were tough lessons. Huge lessons. But he completed the process on the other side. Wow.

Now some may ask, well did you ask about the karma between you and Tom. I had already been repeatedly told that we had none, so I wasn't concerned. For instance, Donna had said,

- *you two are clean*
- *there is only love between you*
- *it is a very deep profound love*

For me the understanding of resolved karma was huge. Tom completed the lessons he struggled to learn on this side AND it took the pressure off me to complete the learning of everything I needed to learn on this side.

Historically, whenever I went to psychics, I asked if I had resolved the karmic lessons I came here to learn. Now it doesn't matter if I have resolved them or not, what is important is whether I **engage** in the process. Big lesson.

Chapter 10

How Do We Learn on the Other Side?

I wanted to understand how Tom was learning his stuff on the other side. Obviously, he didn't go to an academic or trade school. But how does one learn on the other side?

Tom claims that we don't really "learn" on that side, we work at becoming more aware. Well at least that's one thing that psychologists got right on this side. Awareness is a huge component. Awareness and remembering what we have already learned is the key.

At one point, he said,

But remember as I said before, we are not learning this stuff...we are remembering it. We have done this before.

He also said,

Thought is different here too. We can communicate more telepathically – but that is a simple term for a wide variety of communications. And I understand now what you mean about thinking without words...that didn't make sense to me on that side, but now it does.

And I have seen how it slows you down when you have to put words to your thoughts. But there is more to it than that here. *Thinking, processing, learning, remembering are all different, there are more components or variations or aspects or something than they do over there. When we get better at this, I might be able to share that with you...don't know how right now.*

At another time, I asked him to explain again,

I don't know. I just find myself there and realize that it is different. Then I start to explore and experience and somehow, I just know, or a guide shows up and explains.

So, are you meeting more guides?

I think so. Again, I am not sure if that is the right term. But there are other energies that work with me. That help me to understand. Its kind of like having different versions of you with me.

On that side, you were always helping me dig deeper or look at things from different perspectives or become aware of who I was or what I was doing or why I was doing...I loved those conversations. Didn't always like what I saw but I loved that kind of learning. And I continue to get that here. Obviously, it's with other beings...but

You stopped, but what?

I was trying to think what it was...with you, we sat and talked, and you pushed or probed or asked. But here, the learning is different somehow, I am trying to think how it occurs. It's experiential. It is not through conversation in the same way we had conversations...I am thinking of the road trip and the phenomenal conversations we had there or on the cruise ship...some of those conversations we got pretty deep and intense and emotional...but it is different here. The learning is more expansive.

Don't say anything...I am still working on it. I'm not really sure what I am trying to say. You just move into this state of awareness. There is no judgment with it. All the judgment on this side is self judgement. But you see and hear and experience the lesson.

Can you give me an example?

Well, think of my ex...I gave up my power, my control, my identity with her. That started with my Dad when I was a kid. Really, it started in prior lives with both of them. They had both been very abusive in prior lives and I had given up control as a way of coping.

One of the lessons, I came into this life with, was to resolve that control. But I didn't realize what I was doing until you started showing me. I allowed them both to define who I was. You came along and made me define me. That was an awesome gift. One of so many that you gave me.

Tom went on to explain how his guides helped him open up to the awareness of the dynamics; the part he played in it; the contracts he had made with them and with himself before coming into this life. It all came back to awareness. No teaching, discussing, exploring, just awareness.

Tom explained learning again,

Thinking is also very different. You were always trying to get me to think, in different ways, and to come at things from different perspectives...I remember in the Seattle Market giving you a bad time because you wouldn't just agree with me about the cars and parking...you had to give a different perspective (he was frustrated with the drivers, and I attempted to get him to understand where the drivers might be coming from)...

Well, thinking is really even more different here too. Its about awareness more than thinking. You would like it. I'm hoping I can teach you. There are many things I hope to teach you.

And at a later time,

Thinking is very different here, at least for me. As you have noticed I can think on a huge number of levels simultaneously without having to switch back and forth from one thought to another. Thinking is about information and awareness and manifestation. Apparently, it is even more so at higher levels. But I get a big taste of it here.

Yet at another time, he said,

Yes, because I am learning how to learn on this side…remember that it is more about awareness than learning like we understood it on your side…so I have been able to see or be aware of the issues with my Dad and with my ex through out many lives…I have seen how they accumulated – that's not the best word – but how they evolved and impacted on each of us….

Or when he said,

Because I engaged in those lessons and because of the exploration we did, I did a lot of learning which allowed for me more awareness and learning on this side.

He also said,

I am learning to see and feel them as opposed to hear them. (He was talking about his guides) I'm increasing my sense of awareness and with awareness comes learning and understanding.

At another time, he said,

Awareness is huge over here. I know you were always talking about learning how to be more aware, but awareness takes on a whole different meaning over here. 3D awareness is incredibly limited compared to awareness on this side. It should have an entirely different word. It's not just the difference between kindergarten and university, it's more like the difference between knowing how to build a house and understanding marine biology. It is hugely different.

He also said,

Learning just to be is big in and of itself... although I think that is easier for me than it is going to be for you, you are always so busy and you do so much in such a short time I am was always amazed at what you could accomplish... and you are able to and do meditate but learning just to be is different...even different from what I knew on that side. Although on that side, just being was difficult because my anxieties and fears would get in the way and you know what I did to cope with all of that.

But I think I have an easier time learning to be than you will. That is going to be a big lesson for you.

On the other hand, you don't mind being by yourself and with yourself and you have more self acceptance than I did – so maybe it will be easier for you. Just being means you have to be with yourself and accept who you are and be with your lessons – you are better at that than I was so maybe it will be easier for you...certainly different than what I have to learn. It is an amazing experience to just simply accept and love who you are.

Yes, you did try to help me learn to accept myself; define who I was and not let others define me; maybe you laid the foundation for what I am learning now...thank you...

All in all, I think we get the picture that learning, on the other side, is about increasing one's awareness.

I had to laugh. When I did my Ayurveda internships in India, I repeatedly heard people laughing at the psychology "concepts" in the Western world, or in particular, in North America. They were always laughing at how limited our understanding of the mind, consciousness and awareness was.

Now I wonder if their understanding of awareness is more like what Tom is experiencing on the other side. Who knows.

Regardless, the lesson we need to take here is that learning does occur on the other side, but it is done through increasing one's awareness.

Chapter 11

Choices

The lesson of Awareness leads into the lesson of Choices. The more aware we become, the more we become aware of the choices we make.

Let's take a look at these levels of awareness:

1) At the most simplistic level, it is about just doing, without awareness. Not being aware of your emotions, thoughts, behaviours or why you engage them. Simply existing without much self awareness.
2) At a little more advanced level, we can make our own choices or let others make our choices for us.
    a. A particular example of this, is doing what is dictated to us by our family or peers or by an organization or the given culture we live in. Even when we know in our heart of hearts, it is wrong or ineffective or not the best for us, we allow the outside world to dictate to us.
    b. Or not standing up and acknowledging or confronting falsehoods or lies or illusions etc. – out of fear. You know it will be at a cost to you – in the short term. Although

never in the long term of the soul's development.

3) At a more advanced level, we can choose to engage in our lessons that we set out for ourselves before we entered this particular plane of experience, even though they may seem challenging. Too often, it is easier to just give up, or easier to ignore, avoid or deny, etc.

Consequently, we have choices. We can choose to be average, mediocre or we can choose to reach towards our greatest potential – whatever that may be.

Tom struggled with this. He always wanted to be more than what he was. He struggled to learn and grow and hold onto higher truths. He was getting better and better at it and I loved him for it. Watching how he struggled to be a better person and reach his higher potential was always a motivator for me to do the same.

Attempting to unlearn old ineffective habits and replace them with good healthy thoughts and beliefs, emotions and reactions, coping skills, etc. is a challenging road. Especially when those old behaviors were coping mechanisms you used to deal with life, the people around you, and in particular, yourself. We feel great when we embrace new behaviors, and yet it is so easy to slip back into old patterns.

It doesn't seem to matter whether it is our beliefs about ourselves or the ongoing dialogues we have in our head, or how we cope with people in our lives, or a thousand other issues we may have to deal with. Old habits are challenging to change. At least I think most of us find it so.

There is an old saying, that goes along the lines of, "You know when someone is moving out ahead of the rest, by the "arrows" they have in their back". Sometimes it takes a lot of courage to move past the confines, restrictions, beliefs or dictates of various groups, whether that be family and friends, businesses, associations or governments. And, those who do, have the "arrows" in their back to prove it.

Sometimes people believe, they can create or provoke a difference by superficially agreeing with the "group" and creating changes from within. Sometimes people believe they have to be aggressive in order to provoke change and growth. Sometimes people believe they have to stand up within an activist group. People like Gandhi said, "Be the change you want to see." People like Gandhi provoked people to make the change within. There are many ways to create and provoke change both within ourselves and in the culture around us.

Usually, it is a challenge whether you are focusing on internal change or external change. But all the power to you if you believe that you are growing and learning and developing your greater potential by creating change for the better, however you chose to do it.

As Tom experienced the process, it was a challenging road, but it didn't stop him from pursuing it. He did like to remind himself with Gandhi's quotes.

As an aside, the following is a short list of some of Mahatma Gandhi's other notable sayings. They are not in order of priority, simply alphabetically.

"Always aim at complete harmony of thought and word and deed. Always aim at purifying your thoughts and everything will be well."

"An eye for eye only ends up making the whole world blind."

"An ounce of practice is worth more than tons of preaching."

"As human beings, our greatness lies not so much in being able to remake the world – that is the myth of the atomic age – as in being able to remake ourselves."

"Constant development is the law of life, and a man who always tries to maintain his dogmas in order to appear consistent drives himself into a false position."

"First they ignore you, then they laugh at you, then they fight you, then you win."

"Happiness is when what you think, what you say, and what you do are in harmony."

"I claim to be a simple individual liable to err like any other fellow mortal. I own, however, that I have humility enough to confess my errors and to retrace my steps."

"I do not want to foresee the future. I am concerned with taking care of the present. God has given me no control over the Moment following."

"I look only to the good qualities of men. Not being faultless myself, I won't presume to probe into the faults of others."

"I suppose leadership at one time meant muscles; but today it means getting along with people."

"If I had no sense of humor, I would long ago have committed suicide."

"It is unwise to be too sure of one's own wisdom. It is healthy to be reminded that the strongest might weaken and the wisest might err."

"Man becomes great exactly in the degree in which he works for the welfare of his fellow-men."

"Nobody can hurt me without my permission."

"The difference between what we do and what we are capable of doing would suffice to solve most of the world's problems."

"The weak can never forgive. Forgiveness is the attribute of the strong."

"You must be the change you want to see in the world."

"You must not lose faith in humanity. Humanity is an ocean; if a few drops of the ocean are dirty, the ocean does not become dirty."

As much as I have often heard that we come to earth or this plane of existence because it offers us choices or free choice. It seemed to me that Tom still has choices on the other side.

He talked of how everyone has a different pathway. How he thought he was working harder than most. So, I asked if he had free choice on the other side. He said,

Yes, definitely.

Hmmm.

Chapter 12

Learning to Own Your Stuff, Not Theirs

A big lesson that Tom needed to learn on this side but completed on that side, was to let someone else's stuff be their stuff. An important lesson for many of us on this side.

Too often people learn that they are responsible for making someone else happy. Or that they were responsible if someone was upset. This was a huge issue for Tom on this side. I often said to Tom, "It's my issue, not yours. You don't need to take it on or deal with it, it's my stuff."

I remember one time, Tom gave me a beautiful card and, in the card, he wrote out all the things he was thankful to me for. It was beautiful except for one line, "Thank you for all the T&A, you are always so thoughtful."

T&A? I was astounded and dreadfully hurt. We had company that night and I couldn't address it. I didn't know how to address it. Is that what he thought of our relationship. And how could he possibly imbed that, in such a beautiful card.

When we went to bed that night, I curled up on the side of the bed, wanting to cry. I didn't know what to say or how to handle it. I finally took a deep breath and asked, "Is that how you see our relationship, as T&A?"

Tom responded with, "What are you talking about, what a horrible thing to say."

"But that's what you wrote in the card."

"I did not. I would never say something like that."

I took the card off the night table and showed him. I was struggling not to cry, but I was so hurt.

He read the card out to me, it read tea, not T&A. Tom was so hurt that I would think he wrote that. But what was even more interesting was that he was so apologetic for his handwriting. He saw it as being entirely his fault and his poor handwriting that had caused me distress.

We had a long discussion about how it was my fault for misreading it and I should have known what he was writing. How he shouldn't take responsibility for my mis-reading what he wrote. He had written this long beautiful expose on all the things he loved and was thankful for! I was the one who screwed up!!

While he said he understood and agreed, the next day he apologized again and then he texted another apology later in the day.

It made a point of how much he felt responsible for another person's stuff. He felt he was entirely responsible for causing me the hurt. He didn't misread the card, I did. I was the one who needed to be apologetic!!

On one of the trips we took, when we were still just friends, Tom did something that really triggered me. His action was reminiscent of my ex, who would do the behavior but with intent to hurt me. I knew Tom had no intent to hurt me. It was me who was reacting to an old situation.

I worked really hard throughout the day to deal with it without it impacting on Tom. That night I apologized to Tom if I came across with any moodiness during the day. He said he didn't know what I was talking about and wanted to understand. I explained the situation to him without telling him what the actual behavior was. I didn't want him to know and become overly self aware.

But he apologized for upsetting me. I explained again, it wasn't him, it was me and I was the one apologizing. He apologized three times the next day for upsetting me. I had to keep explaining that it wasn't his fault, it was my stuff, my issue. He had nothing to apologize for. But again, he had learned in life that everything was always his fault and he was responsible for making everyone else happy. He was of no value, if someone else wasn't happy!!!

Now let's take that reference and understand the following. One of the times I went to see Terry, I had a list of questions I needed answered. Things Tom had said to me or things that Terry had relayed that I wanted more clarification with. They both tease me that I am forever asking for more clarification…

On the way to her office, I asked Tom to be as up front with me and the questions as he could be. "Please don't sugar coat anything, just give it to me straight."

Well he did. For most of the session, I understood. It provided a number of levels of understanding that I hadn't understood previously, but there was one line in the 1.5-hour session that really threw me for a loop.

When I left Terry's, I had a really tough time with it. I was angry with Tom and in tears. I didn't know how to deal with it. I knew it was my issue, not his. It was something I was not prepared for and it really threw me sideways.

Tom was upset that I was so upset. He wanted to help me work it through. He didn't understand why I was so upset.

I kept pushing him away, telling him to leave me alone. It was my issue and I needed to deal with it on my own. I finally told him to "F*** Off", something I never did, with anyone! I told him, I loved him, and I would continue to work with him, but right now he had to go away and leave me alone while I worked through this one.

It was a difficult issue for me. Terry and I texted back and forth over the next couple of days, as I struggled to deal with it. Suzanna and Katherine also struggled to help me deal with it. They both understood where I was coming from and were incredibly understanding and supportive.

Finally, I found a way of dealing with it and resolving it. Then I was able to connect with Tom again.

Tom's response was,

That's why you never get stuck in emotional drama. You push through it and work it until you resolve it. Actually, I can see how others might think it is emotional drama in the Moment if they don't understand what you are actually doing with it. But you do move through it quickly. Once again, you are amazing.

I was having a difficult time with it on this side. Hated to see you suffer like you did and to know that I, in a sense caused it. I am not responsible for your reactions, but I provided the input, if you will. And I love you and I am sorry that my input caused that or provoked you that way.

But to sit and watch what you did with it was an amazing exercise for me. I had to have the empathy and understanding for what you were going through without taking responsibility for your reaction – only the input. On that side, because of my childhood and how I learned to respond to my Dad and to my ex – I would have taken full responsibility for your reaction.

I wanted to be there for you and support you through it, but I didn't take responsibility for it. That was really different for me. It was like I found a piece of myself again. A piece that I had lost through various lifetimes.

I came really close to taking responsibility for it when I saw your reactions to my choice of words. I think that maybe, part of what you went through, was for my benefit. I needed to learn that piece. It was huge for me.

If you didn't go through your process, I couldn't have gone through mine.

So, then I started to feel guilty that you were suffering, so that I could go through my crap, in reaction. But my guides, especially my Mom, helped me through it. And I stayed grounded, so to speak, with my lesson.

It is amazing to learn that your Mom is actually, like a spiritual guide. She was so helpful.

Anyways, she knew how much I needed to learn from and with you and that is why she guided us back together on that side.

It is amazing to see how many of the issues we went through on that side, and now with me on this side, are so intertwined. We agreed to them previously. So, in a sense it makes it easier for me than for you, because I now have that awareness.

So just know that. We both agreed to the processes and learning that we are doing. I have told you before how intertwined we are – it just goes very deep.

We got sidetracked onto other issues, but Tom came back to the discussion.

On that side, I would have been so afraid of losing you watching or knowing what you were going through. On this side, there was no fear. I had to be patient and I had to stay grounded and work through my stuff, but there was more than that.

I have always trusted that when you held me accountable it was for my own good. Well usually, sometimes I had to remind myself because it would get twisted up with my ex, but I had that trust. That trust goes far deeper now. Maybe that's a reflection of my love for you going deeper, just thought of that. Maybe it's because I am on this side. Maybe it's because even as you went through your stuff and pushed me away, you still told me that you loved me and to be patient with you.

Seeing how you struggled to come from a higher place was amazing and that with all the hurt you still loved me was amazing. But again, it's more than even that. Like you, there are times that I am at a loss for words to describe what I am feeling.

Again, Tom got sidetracked, but came back again.

Maybe that is part of it, even emotions are different over here. The love is more intense and full. But even saying that, I love you more now than when I was first here. That in and of itself is growing. There is a peace with it. Maybe that's it. There is a peace and trust with it that just stays through everything. Does that make sense to you?

The following week, he came back again to the events of the week and what he learned.

But I still have stuff I need to learn. You really threw me last week. I thought that I was stronger than I was but you going through your crap as you call it – really made me question me.

That I could cause you that much pain and suffering, stirred up stuff that I wasn't good enough...I had to really look at that and keep grounded in that I may have provided the data, but you had to work through your own crap to process it. We both had a tough a week. And rather than run away from it...I stayed with it...but that also meant I had to deal with you pushing me away, so you could work through it. It was tough.

In my mind, this is a huge lesson that so many of us need to learn. How and when to let someone else's stuff be their stuff. As a psychologist, and as a person, it was a common issue that I had to address with people on this side.

Understanding when it is your stuff versus their stuff; understanding that you may have provided the input, but that they are responsible for their reaction; or accepting that it is just their stuff. The ability to differentiate and accept when it is us and when it is them. A huge lesson.

Tom had a difficult time with this lesson on this side, but he obviously learned what he needed to on the other side. Why? Because he had engaged in this lesson on this side.

We have talked several times since then about whether or not at some level, I had agreed to go through my "hell" so that he could work through his lesson of letting it be my stuff. Once I worked through it, it didn't seem so big. I chastised myself because I knew the variables that surrounded it and I shouldn't have had such a big reaction. Yet, when I was in it, it was huge and incredibly hurtful.

Tom was then able to take the lesson and apply it to his ex.

To let her stuff be her's.

I am not responsible, I am not to blame.

I don't need to feel guilty.

I don't need to see her or be with her or watch her journey in any way.

I just need to work on letting other people's stuff be theirs, including my Dad's and her's.

Yeah, I can see that thought in your mind – that is what you were always trying to teach me. You seemed to have got that lesson better than I did. I saw how you worked that through with your Mom.

Letting all her criticisms and judgements be a reflection of who she was and not of you...I have seen all your hurt and pain over that and how you worked it through.

I don't need to connect with them anymore to work it through...I just need to do work on it within me."

The lesson, is that we need to let other people's stuff be their stuff...and Tom learned the lesson. And he learned the lesson on the other side. Again, perhaps because he had attempted to engage in the process on this side.

Chapter 13

Learning to Just Be

One morning, I questioned Tom, "What is the learning you are doing on that side?"

Learning just to be is big in and of itself...although I think that is easier for me than it is going to be for you, you are always so busy, and you do so much in such a short time. I am always amazed at what you could accomplish...and you are able to, and do, meditate but learning just 'to be' is different...even different from what I knew on that side. Although on that side, 'just being' was difficult for me because my anxieties and fears would get in the way and you know what I did to cope with all of that.

But I think I have an easier time learning 'to be' than you will. That is going to be a big lesson for you.

On the other hand, you don't mind being by yourself and with yourself and you have more self acceptance than I did – so maybe it will be easier for you. "Just being" means you have to be with yourself and accept who you are and be with your lessons – you are better at that than I was so maybe it will be easier for you...certainly different than what I have to learn. It is an amazing experience to just simply accept and love who you are.

Yes, you did try to help me learn to accept myself; define who I was and not let others define me; maybe you laid the foundation for what I am learning now...thank you.

I think many people, myself included, allow business and the 'doingness of life' to get in the way of 'just being'. I work at compensating for that with meditation as well as all the different types of exercises, like working with OBEs, or astral travel or Merkabah.

I know one could argue, that while I am relaxed and focused and meditating or whatever, that I am also busy attempting to learn or do something. But at the same time, I can argue, that it is time spent going within and being, as opposed to, the doingness on the outside.

Whichever way you want to look at it, apparently it is an important lesson, and one we continue to work with on the other side. So, it must be pretty important.

Chapter 14

Emotions on the Other Side

Emotions are tricky things. For many years, I have believed that emotions are one of three gifts we are given: thoughts, emotions and behaviors. We can develop these three gifts, or we can allow them to control us, i.e., 'analysis can cause paralysis', 'emotions can cause distortions' and 'behaviors can run us amuck'.

Developing our intellect is about developing upper management cognitive skills like critical analysis, objective perspective, evaluative skills, differential analysis, etc., NOT collecting a data bank. People often confuse having a lot of information with being intelligent. They are quite different. Rote memory is one of the lowest forms of intelligence and involves simple memorization of data.

Likewise, people often misunderstand emotional development. Developing emotionally is not about coming from a positive place but rather learning ***not*** to judge the emotion, or the self for having the emotion. Emotions are simply emotions, without being negative or positive. We attribute the positive or negative interpretation to them, when we shouldn't.

We are meant to be emotional beings. We come here to have emotional experiences. We talked of fear in an earlier chapter. Fear can either prevent us from embracing who we are, or fear can keep us alive. For instance, if you are a single female walking through a dangerous area of downtown in the dark, fear may be a good asset. It will provoke you to be more aware; move quickly to a place of safety; or react defensively when needed. On the other hand, fear can also paralyze you, so that you can't move. Thus, the fear is neither negative or positive, but rather how and when you use it determines whether is effective or ineffective.

Anger can also work for you or against you. There is one person in my life that I experienced a lot of anger with. I had to move through the anger and resolve it and let it go. BUT, I know that if I am really tired and still have to keep working, I can step back into that place of anger; get my adrenals going; and finish the day's work. In my mind, I learned to use the anger effectively.

So, emotions can be tricky. If we judge them, they can be a detriment. If we don't understand and recognize them, they can also be a detriment. If we give them full range of control, they can be a detriment. However, when we are charge of them, and learn to use them wisely, then they are a benefit.

So, we need to learn how to recognize and own our emotions; not judge, repress, avoid or deny emotions. We need to allow the self to experience them without judging the self for experiencing them; and release them and let them go. A good exercise is learning to be the "Objective Bystander" to the emotion.

I have often said that the emotion I do best, is hurt. Not because I enjoy the hurt emotion, but rather because it is very familiar and easy to go there. I grew up in a household where you were not allowed to be angry. You were never allowed to raise your voice; or do any of the normal "angry" behaviors. So, I learned to stay in the hurt.

Neither Tom nor I were good at anger. But for entirely different reasons. I just explained why I had a difficult time with anger. But for Tom, it was entirely different. He was afraid of anger. Afraid of what it did to people and how it could hurt people. So, he stayed with the hurt rather than get angry.

Thus, we both tended to avoid anger by getting stuck in our hurt.

One of Tom's comments from the other side was,

You also had to forgive me, for hurting you in this life, and again, it is not like I did it with intent either.

But also, from prior lives. You don't hold resentment, but you hold the hurt. You always said that you did hurt better than any other emotion...now I understand why you say that.

But you need to understand it as well and let it go. I remember you telling me about that bizarre meditation when you were at the University of Connecticut and the huge hurt process you went through with that...don't let it build up again...let it go. Fill it with love."

Another time, he said,

Because of the learning I did on that side with you and because of the learning I did on this side, I started operating like you and really embraced the learning. I didn't avoid it. You taught me how to confront issues and I don't know that I ever confronted them in the same way on this side before. I don't know maybe I did. But it felt like I gained a lot more this time, than I had before. I think it was because of or reflective of the learning I did on that side with you. Maybe? I guess I'm not really sure just yet.

Lots of work still to do. I am thinking that maybe before I was afraid of emotions, even on this side. Whereas you taught me not to be afraid of them.

Its not like I couldn't cry on that side, I was just afraid of going into them (the emotions) and understanding them. Maybe that's it. You pushed me to go deeper. Actually, you didn't even push me...you invited me. You allowed me to do it in a safe way with understanding and compassion.

I think we did that in a prior life as well. When we were in that lifetime where we were married, you and I had a good capacity to take each other deeper. But that was more about just us, whereas this time you helped me go deeper with regard to other people or in other relationships.

I don't know, does all this make sense to you?"

Yes, it certainly did. And it is a good lesson, don't be afraid of your emotions. Work with them. They are a gateway or a door to helping you work through and resolve stuff.

But perhaps, an even more interesting aspect of emotion, is that those on the other side can experience our emotions.

At one point, Tom said,

You know I am always here...even when I am elsewhere doing other things, I am still here with you. I feel your emotions as you go through them.

Or when he said,

I want you to know how much I love you

He also said,

Just like when I feel your intent when you stroke my picture. I feel your intent and I feel your emotions.

Another time, he said,

Its just interesting to be able to feel your emotions. As opposed to interpret them from my perspective on that side. Its just different. Its like I understand you better and where you are coming from."

He also said, that we can provoke emotions in those on the other side,

I know you try to help everyone...you always did...and I know you try to get them to help themselves as well...you were always good at that.

Wow...that just provoked emotion in me and how much I appreciated how you worked at getting me to help myself and to define myself, by myself and all the other stuff we did. I hope you know how much I appreciated it then and still appreciate it now...there is a reason you are my true love...

Another way of looking at emotions, comes from what he said during the time I was going through some of my hurt.

You need to go through it. Remember what you always told me...its neither good nor bad...just emotion...allow it to be ...just experience it and let it go...you are good at that...you don't need to worry about replacing it with love...you have the love...so simply allow the emotion to be ...you came to experience it so experience it...and then let it go.

You are so full of love right now...that just shows how much love you have even when you experience the hurt.

Yes, and the laughter. You know how you love it when I laugh, well I get a similar high when I feel you laughing. We did well with all the emotions from love and laughter to hurt...although neither of us did anger well...we both would drown in our hurt rather than get angry.

Yes, I saw those memories...make up hugs...we did those well too...for hours...thank you so much for those...I needed them so much just to hold you and cuddle like that meant the world to me you have no idea.

Wow. Its interesting from this side, I can feel, understand, (and) empathize what different experiences were for you. Sometimes you experienced things so differently than I did and other times you experienced things virtually the same as me. I love understanding your experiences from this side. You were a lot better at that than me.

I love you. Know that. It is important. You don't always know that. You need to. Focus on it. It is important. The more you can appreciate, feel, (and) experience how much I really love you, the easier it will be for you to move through the hurt. So, experience it and at the same time experience my love. Do both.

A whole other aspect of emotions that Tom taught me, was about the Emotional Portals that connect our chakras to our upper layers of DNA – he explained that in the second book: <u>Tom: Cosmic Healing</u>.

I think the lessons here about emotions might be:

- They are neither good nor bad
- We are neither good nor bad for experiencing them
- We can affect those on the other side with the emotions we experience here – not sure if that is the case if we are *not* connected with them
- And we can provoke an emotional kind of experience in those on the other side

Chapter 15

Lessons About Healing

This is a big and important chapter for me. My whole life has been about helping people heal and learn, on all levels of life. It is something I resonated with, from kindergarten on. I love to teach, and I love all the different healing modalities, so it came naturally. I have also been told by spiritual masters that 'teaching and healing' are my life purpose – that makes sense to me.

But I have to admit, I didn't like med school. Couldn't believe how far behind they were and that most of it was based on hypotheses, not on real evidence, as is commonly believed and marketed. And the fact that we are all so different really plays havoc with the "normal curve" hypothesis that MDs are taught to use.

As much as I learned a lot in Naturopathic College, in my mind, they just didn't go far enough. On the other hand, they would probably all think I am really nuts if they were aware of what I have written with Tom. Oh well.

I was always amazed at how much Tom was interested in the work I did and the different healing modalities.

And he really listened. I would hear him explain things to other people, that I had told him years before! Really? You remember all that?

When we were on trips, he was always in conversations with people about what I did; or the books that I had written. I remember one trip we were on; a young woman came over and joined us at our picnic table as we were eating lunch.

She was lovely and was a song writer and musician. She claimed that she could see our energy and that we had a fascinating energy and claimed that the love between us must be very deep. So, she decided to serenade us for about 45 minutes with a few of her songs. It was lovely.

Anyways, her back was achy and sore. While I was packing up our' lunch stuffs', Tom went into the car and put a topical lotion together for her back. I listened to him explain what he was doing and why and what Holly had taught him to do for himself. He always made sure that I knew exactly what he was doing to make sure that he was doing it correctly, I rarely ever had to correct him. As usual, I thought he was awesome. And of course, he was. And he still is.

Anyways, because Tom was always so intrigued with what I did; respected my work to the nth degree; came to conferences when I presented; shared the information with other people; it seemed rather logical that we are so entwined and share a mutual interest in helping people heal. And because we also both had a fascination with spiritual development, the following made sense.

Terry said,

- *It is also important to both of you to help people to heal and prepare for ascension"*

At a later point, Terry said,

- *There is a need to project new meaning into the healing aspect of universal energy*
- *He has been chosen to work with you to provide a new outlook in the healing process*
- *12 colors; energies; you will produce it together"*

At another session, she said,

- *He showed me:*
- *Visualize*
- *A host of colours*
- *All represent something different*
- *Feel more colors in various directions*
- *Each color and direction has a meaning*
- *A healing aspect to each*
- *Everything he sees has specific colors*
- *Everything is done in incredible colors*
- *If there isn't color – there is something wrong*

When Tom talks about healing, he is not just referring to the physical, or the psychological or the spiritual as we generally think of it. Tom talks about turning on the twelve Layers of DNA. He claims that most of it is turned off for most of us. But there are a variety of ways we can turn it on. He explains this in his book, Tom: Cosmic Healing.

Apparently, there are more books to come, but I have no idea what they will be about at present. I have no idea if the next will get written this year or next year or in the next decade. So far, I learn about each book when he decides we need to write another one. And, apparently, he works with his guides to determine that.

I am not concerned, as I still need to complete my "Entwined" book series". You might say, Tom interrupted my agenda with his!

Tom just told me what the next book will be about. That's really funny. Okay, so I have a weird sense of humor.

I started to laugh and said, "They are going to have to wait."

Tom laughed as well, saying, "I knew you were going to say that."

Anyways, according to Tom, one of the aspects of healing on the other side, has to do with increasing awareness and/or remembering. In fact, he suggests that awareness is a big part of healing on this side as well. It is the first step to real healing.

Chapter 16

What We Take with Us

One aspect I found interesting with Tom, on the other side, was how much of his personality he took with him.

Tom always had a great sense of humor. I probably thought that because our humor was very similar. I think that is probably the same with most people, we enjoy another's humor when it is similar to our own. We had a great time laughing and kibitzing. And Tom certainly took that sense of humor with him.

As explained in his first book, Tom: Cosmic Socialite, I went through a lot of self doubt and self questioning, in the early stages of this new kind of relationship. Was this really Tom I was feeling, hearing and sometimes seeing? Or was this just my mind making everything up to help me deal with the grieving? Tom's humor helped a lot.

I would start talking and he would interrupt me. Now Tom was the type who never interrupted when you talked, unless he was having fun with you. And here he was, on the other side, having fun struggling to convince me that it was really him by interrupting me.

Another time, when I was at a weekend workshop, he apparently thought I was getting too serious and he started tickling me. Now how do you explain to the people around you that someone, from the other side, is tickling you?

If he wants to make a comment to someone, usually a friend, and wants to get my attention, he will kiss me. Always gets my attention! And lately, several different friends have commented, asking something along the lines of, "What did Tom just do?" or "Did Tom just kiss you?" It is amazing how many people are starting to pick up energetic information who never did before.

As much as we have a lot of serious, heavy duty conversations in the mornings, we also have many conversations that are just really lighthearted and fun.

I am very appreciative of all the laughter that we still share. It always makes my heart sing to hear him laughing. It is a strange thing to "hear" or "feel" someone laugh on the other side, and even more difficult to describe, but it still feels good.

Another aspect that Tom carried with him, was his consideration. Tom was always a very considerate person on this side and he maintains that on the other side. Typically, Tom wakes me up in the early hours to work on "energy work", OBEs, Merkaba, etc. But, if I am tired and need to sleep, he doesn't wake me up. He lets me sleep. I so appreciate that.

Tom was always great for my ego. I am thankful that while he was on this side, we were always very appreciative, grateful and acknowledging of one another.

My Dad and I made plaques for Mom & Tom to put in the garden at the new house. My plaque for Tom, reads:

> Thank you for being you
> Thank you for loving me
> Thank you for continuing to be

The first two lines are out of respect of the lines that Tom and I said to one another regularly. Tom is still very loving with lines like that. He is still so appreciative of what I shared with him while he was on this side. Perhaps even more so, considering it helped him to engage in the lessons he needed to learn and was able to resolve on the other side. I am anxious to see what I get to resolve or complete on the other side thanks to Tom.

Tom was a very gentle, loving, affectionate man on this side and he still is on the other side. Whether he is pushing me to do the work; or cuddling me at night; or putting his arm around me when I am crying, struggling to come from a place of abundance rather than lack; he is always there, loving and gentle and affectionate.

And he still holds me accountable with fun. He always liked finding things he could hold me accountable for, it made him feel good and always made him laugh. His brother started calling him a Jedi Master some time ago, and we have played with it ever since…

Yes, oh great Jedi Master, I hear you giving me shit…and I look up at your pictures and I am taken straight away to the one where you are grinning at me…with that look I know so well…oh well.

Hey, I am not giving you shit…I was just reminding you…but I love it when you call me a Jedi Master…that came from my brother, I remember…but it is funny…maybe one day we will both be Jedi Masters…in the meantime…I saw your reminder for the show…way you go…talk later.

Thanks, love ya.

I always said that Tom's underlying life themes were about fun and adventure. And he is having a lot of fun and adventure on other side. Both with me and on his own.

When talking about dreaming, Tom made the following comment,

I know I don't always connect with you at night. I have tried to figure out why sometimes it is easier than others but haven't figured that out yet. I like dreaming with you, its fun. Its like an adventure because I am in different frequencies then.

We were talking about an energetic shift one time, and Tom said the following,

There was a shift that occurred last night. It affected me too. I don't know if you realize that when I crossed over there was a huge sense of loss for me too. There was the physical loss of you. I stayed connected with you

energetically which was awesome, that is difficult for most people.

And even when they do get that, it isn't for a period of time. But we had it immediately, but there was still the loss of you physically. And now I had to work at connecting with you. I couldn't just text or call through the day or be there in the evening or through the night. I had to really work at it.

And of course, there was my guilt for having left you...I really didn't mean to leave you...you were the one good thing in my life...you were what kept me grounded... even in the midst of all the other crap that was going on. You were my laughter and my adventure and my fun and my connection to life and to my higher self. And then all of a sudden, I was here and had to figure things out without you.

It was a journey and an adventure, and you were always a huge part of it, but as you know, it is still different. And you are right, we need to learn to come from a place of abundance and not lack. But it is still a huge adjustment. I thank you again for being so loving and compassionate and supportive along the way. I don't know what I would have done without you...as always. I am glad we are such a strong team."

When discussing this new relationship we are in, Tom also saw it as an adventure,

You were always great at celebrating everything about life. I even started enjoying our monthly anniversaries... at first it was just weird, and I didn't know what to do with it. But you made it simple and easy and it was fun. And yes, we can celebrate our lives and how far we have come in 7 months. We have had quite a journey. Or an adventure and you know how I always loved adventures.

The fact that we are connecting across dimensions is huge and what we are accomplishing is huge. At least for us. There are those who are much further ahead, there always will be. And that is good. But we are doing great and, so we need or can chose to celebrate us and our connection across dimensions. And we can do that celebration in your sense of time. We are celebrating our new-found relationship. Even though we have been together for many many eons, we can celebrate this aspect of the journey or the adventure. So Happy Anniversary My Love.

What a guy. You gotta love it. Especially if you are a romantic like me. It sure helped me start looking at his crossing over, differently. So yes, we have a wonderful new adventure, and we celebrate our monthly anniversaries, both the original one and the new one. Yeah, I know, I'm nuts. What can I say?

Tom was always struggling to grow and learn and meet his greater potential on this side. We both worked at it in a wide variety of ways. As with most, it was a struggle with many ups and downs, but he kept getting up and working at it. And he continues to do so on the other side.

All in all, there are many aspects to our personality that we take with us. I haven't identified anything negative at this point.

Tom just laughed as I wrote that, and said, *"I don't have any negatives characteristics."* Again, his sense of humor coming through.

Of course not!

Chapter 17

What we Learn on the Other Side

I am not sure of all that we learn on the other side. I would think that that is as unique and individual as the lessons we each come in with to learn on this side. And unlike Tom, I don't have the vast awareness and recall that he has. I am still limited to this lifetime.

So, all I can really share is what I know about Tom and what he has told me.

We have already identified that if we engage in the lessons we come here to learn, then we can complete them on the other side. So, that would cover a lot in and of itself.

But I understand that there are many other things we learn as well. For instance, Tom often talks about his increasing awareness and that awareness is the basis of learning.

In addition, he talks about moving through gate ways or portals. From what he tells me, there are many different types of portals. One type involves moving from one dimension to another.

Again, awareness is hugely important here. The awareness involves identifying and shifting one's vibrational frequencies. Those who are more aware and sensitive have the capacity to start that learning on this side.

Tom really enjoys working with the frequencies and moving through these kinds of portals.

I would love to know what you did today…

Well, I floated around in various colors of light and went through a gate of some sort…not sure how to explain it just yet, but it allowed me to raise my vibrations. A guide went through with me and helped me navigate I guess…that's not really a good word for it but I don't know what else to call it.

So, did you do it on your own then?

No, I just went through with her.

Ahhh, so it's a female…that's the first you have mentioned a female other than our mothers…did you or I or we know her in any lifetimes?

I did, I think, way back, but I don't know if you ever did.

Does she have a given function, like my guides do?

Yes, she helps me go through portals or gates by raising my vibrational frequency."

At another time, we had this conversation,

Okay then. Well you know how much I love you and as much as it is difficult to believe, I seem to love you more and more all the time and in different ways or on different levels. It is amazing that it can continue to grow like it does. It's like finding out there are different frequencies that we can attend to and learning to love on those different frequencies. Does that make sense to you?

Yes, that is exactly what it is. I am just capable of experiencing more frequencies than you right now, so I can love you even more...but as you continue the work, you will continue to connect on more and more different frequencies as well. It really is an awesome journey. And we are very fortunate.

And I love you so much. And I love being able to tell you that without all the fears and programs I had on the other side. It is so much more and full of life and it just feels so good. I really really love you in so many ways and with such a depth, it is truly profound.

Thank you, I hope the love that I feel for you has something that you can connect with as well. It feels or sounds like you give me a 120% and I give you a little 10%, but I give you all that I have.

You are funny. All that you have is immense, and I love it and I receive it all with 'graciousness and gratitude' as you would say. And I love it when you feel my love flow through you, I can see it and feel it myself. It is incredibly mutual. We do, do it well.

And now I am supposed to work…how do I work after a session like that?

With love and gratitude, my Susie Q...go to work, I am right here with you, although I will be doing some other stuff today with gates or portals or something...still in the process of becoming more aware...but I am always with you. Just know that."

At another time I asked about the vibrations,

What about the work you were doing raising your vibration, so you can go through the portals or gates or whatever?

Yes, I am working on that as well in a similar manner. The more I can understand about moving through the portals and gates, the better able I will be to come through the gate to you and help you move through the gate to me...I won't say I am trying to learn, I know how you hate the word try or trying...so I will say...I was working at becoming more aware...how's that?"
(Another example of Tom's humor.)

Early in our attempts to communicate, I asked about different types of portals,

And now about my dreams last night. Was that going through portals and am I right in thinking that portals are not just about dimensions and vibrations like I thought, but they can also be about emotional portals?

Yes, that was what I was trying to get across. And you figured it out. Way to go. There are many different types of portals. I didn't know how to explain it and you did it perfectly. That was what I was working on with my Mom.

She actually has a beautiful name on this side, I just don't know how to convey it to you on that side. So, we will continue to call her Mom, I guess. But she has been working with me on going through emotional portals. It helps me address and resolve all the pain I carried not just from this past lifetime but from prior ones.

Again, thanks to the tools that you gave me, she was able to help me work them even further on this side. So, I have been going through the portals and working through the emotions. You would find it fascinating..."

Chapter 18

Connecting with the Other Side

I often get people asking, how does one connect with those on the other side. Usually, these people want to connect with someone in particular, but sometimes it is just out of curiosity. Problem is, I don't know.

When Tom initially crossed over, that very morning I could feel him come up behind me and put his arms around me. On this side, it was usually in the kitchen that he would come up behind and just wrap his arms me. I can remember him saying, so often, "I just love being able to hold you like that." And I loved it too. Once he crossed over, I *felt* him do the same thing throughout the day. I loved it and it just made me cry harder.

By night time I was utterly exhausted from all the grieving emotions throughout the day. Yet during the night, I woke up several times, as I felt his arms curl around me cuddling me. So right then, that very first day, I started questioning my sanity.

I justified it in the early days thinking it was okay, my mind was just working through the grieving and it felt so good, so what the H**l. Although I was sure he was "there" in some sense.

But it started to increase. It became more intense. I saw Tom walk across the kitchen when my Dad and I were playing crib. Then he started pulling stunts that I challenged him with. Then Tom started to talk. At first, it was so faint, and I had a difficult time understanding him. But the more I meditated and concentrated, the easier it was. Then he started to show me pictures of himself. And then once in awhile I got to see him. All this occurred in the first month of Tom crossing over!

It was an odd thing, because on the one hand, I wanted it so much and on the other hand when I got it, I questioned my sanity. As it became more frequent and more intense, I started to go to psychics and mediums and channelers. What were they getting from him? Could they somehow validate my experience?

I couldn't get any kind of validation from my family and friends during that first part of the journey. That would be like going to a friend and asking if they could determine whether or not you had cancer. In that case, I would have to go to physician who would recommend a further specialist, an oncologist.

I also needed to go to a specialist in the field. A psychic. But with many, I questioned their authenticity, so I had to be careful. Also, I needed to go to a specific type of psychic. And, so I went. To a variety of them: psychics, channelers and mediums.

In the beginning, the most powerful medium experience I had, was at the program I spoke of earlier, called 'Messages from the Other Side'. Without even knowing my name, the two mediums acknowledged that both Mom and Tom had crossed over and then that I had sold my house. I think I really started to engage with Tom, at that point.

But why or how, I really don't know. However, if we look at some of the things that Terry said, they might give us a clue:

Terry said,

- *Tom – he is not a guide – he is a soul mate*
- *Travels with you*
- *You have been in prior lives before*
- *Your purpose is very intertwined*
- *Tom wants you to do automatic writing"*

So, it might have to do with:

- Being a soul mate
- Having several lives together
- Having a purpose that is very intertwined
- Tom wanting to do something with me as opposed to me just wanting it

Terry continued on with,

- *Tom is impatient*
- *You share the same vision*

- *Just write and critique later*
- *There will be little to correct*

Further on she said,

- *Allow the humanness to get out of the way*
- *Its amazing (I think she was referring to the book on Healing)*
- *It's a real eye opener*
- *Get involved, get immersed into it*
- *It is a positive*
- *You will understand it*
- *Just go with it*
- *Ask additional questions and you will get answers*
- *Just trust the answers"*

So now in addition, to wanting to see Tom, we also had additional reasons:

- I was curious about what he was going through on the other side
- I was given direction to get involved
- I was given direction to ask questions
- I was told I would get answers

Terry continued on,

- *Tom will help you with the automatic writing, but he will also help you move between dimensions with intent*

- *He will also help you to see him*
- *You will need to work at keeping balance between the different dimensions – ALL WORLDS*
- *You will work with 3-4-5th dimensions*
- *And moving in and out of space*
- *Remember to keep it all balanced*
- *You will see Tom – if you do the work*

Well, there again, we have a number of different issues:

- Tom would help me develop different psychic gifts
- Tom would help me to learn to cross dimensions
- Tom would teach me how to see him – if I did the work

The reasons for me to stay attentive and listen and learn were increasing. Terry continued on:

- *He has a lot more to offer you from the other side*
- *You will continue the journey together*
- *It will change how you operate and how you work with transcendence*
- *You two have a very solid connection*
- *Have been in other lives together*
- *You are very intertwined*
- *He has purpose*
- *Now he sees and knows what his purpose is*
- *He feels strong about it*

- *You help him with his purpose*
- *You are part of his purpose*
- *Part of his purpose is to work through you*
- *He is now manifesting what he needs to manifest, and, on this side, he is manifesting it through you*
- *He will tell you what to write*
- *You need to follow his guidance*

I asked. "What are these gifts he is supposed to be helping me with? "

- *Tom will teach you to travel across space and time and other dimensions*
- *He will teach you to go across different realms with intent*
- *He will teach you to open up to channeling spirit*
- *He will teach you how to access your gifts*
- *He will also teach you to see him*

Later in the session, she said,

- *He is saying: do the damn work – now – just do it*
- *His attention to you is particularly important because you both want to be together*
- *It is also important to both of you to help people to heal and prepare"*

Oh boy, the reasons just kept increasing:

- Tom felt he had more to offer me from the other side – I wanted to know what that was
- The fact that I kept being told we would continue our journey together
- He now had purpose – I knew how important that was for him and the fact that I was part of it, just made me feel good
- That he would work his purpose through me – intrigued me – How? What?
- The fact that he would help me move across dimensions – wow, that was just…I don't know. Sounded awesome? But believable?
- That we would help people heal and ascend – that was just too awesome
- That he wanted me to help do the work

So, it wasn't just that I loved him and wanted to be connected to him, but there was a whole ship load of reasons to be connected. Did all of this help our connection – I would think so.

This line is difficult for me to put in, because I still don't know how I feel about it or what I want to do with it, but Terry claimed that…

- *You two have a very deep connection*
- *You are the only one who can do this*
- *Even the angels – say that you are the right person for this process*
- *He believes in angels*
- *He accepts a lot more than before.*

I will just let you do what you want with that one.

We can also go back to what Tom and I did in this life time, according to what Terry said, Tom said:

I have full trust that you and I worked together while I was there, even on levels we weren't aware of and now while we are on different sides, we can work together even better.

Bottom line about connecting with someone on the other side:

- Does it have to do with having prior lives together?
- Does it have to do with being soul mates?
- Does it have to with the preparation we did on this side?
- Does it have to do with having a joint or entwined purpose?
- Does it have to with the kind of love; or the depth of love; between the two people/souls?
- Does it have to do with just being open minded and allowing?
- Does it have to do with being willing to confront the doubts, the self questioning, and not being afraid of what others might think?

It may be any one of these or any combination of these or it may have to do with entirely different issues that we are not even aware of.

On the other hand, what do any of these issues have to do with him showing up to the realtor or the general contractor and various friends and relatives? I don't know.

So, I asked Tom,

What allows for connection with one person and not another?

Yeah, you hit a number of issues, but there are many more. Whether the person on this side has the ability; or whether there is an agenda or what the agenda is; what stage of processing or learning the person on this side has; and other issues that I don't know how to explain.

And of course, like you said, the beliefs and development of the person on your side; whether they take the time to listen – you had a hard time with that. If I didn't answer right away, your mind travelled elsewhere. I had to learn to connect from this side. I was learning too. Like you, self doubt and self questioning can get in the way for many. Fears, limiting beliefs, all that stuff. But also, what vibrational frequency the person is operating at on your side, is a huge issue, and we still aren't taught any of that on that side.

So, now you have my analysis of the situation from a 3D perspective and you have a summary of Tom's perspective. You will have to decide for yourself what allows or disallows the connection for you.

Chapter 19

Come from a Place of Abundance

In life on this side, we are often taught to come from a place of 'gratitude and appreciation' or to come from a 'place of abundance'. I believe this is an important lesson in life. Certainly, as both a friend and a psychologist, I have always attempted to help people focus on all that they do have, rather than what they don't have or, what they want. There is no problem wanting something, but how we approach might be a part of whether we achieve it or not. For instance, if you want a given career, you need to go after it with determination and145 not let challenges get in the way.

On the other hand, I really want to be able to see Tom with intent. But repeatedly, I have been told that the "wanting" is getting in the way of receiving. Just open up and allow. Don't push it. It will come in its own time. Tom is great for reminding me, don't push, just allow. Frustrating as all get out, but…

For someone who was always taught to "go out and make it happen" or "God helps those who help themselves" or any other of a number of such lines, sitting back and just allowing is challenging. Or, if you want, simply another lesson.

Anyways, I have found out that coming from a place of abundance helps tremendously when going through grieving.

When I focused on the fact that I had "lost" Tom; that he was no longer with me; that I wouldn't be able to feel or see or hear him again, at least in the manner I was used to; that I wouldn't get his hugs or kisses; or come home to him having made dinner served with candle lights and hugs; or all the things that we had planned to do that we would never get to do (we had made a list of all the things we would do for our monthly anniversaries for the next two years and the trips that we wanted to take); that I would no longer get to enjoy romancing with him in a 101 different ways; then I was at a loss. My world crumbled. The pain and anguish would set in and my heart would tear as tears slid down my face and created puddles around me.

If, however, I could come from a place of laughter and fun; be appreciative of the new relationship I had that was growing and developing with Tom; that I could feel and hear his laughter; that I could feel his arms around me and his kisses on my cheek – even though it was entirely different; that I had the growing capacity to converse with him; then my life was both full and fulfilling with all of his love and laughter. Then life was good again. It was full and rewarding, even if very weird.

Nothing outwards changed between the two scenarios, it was only the filtering mechanism I used to interpret the world around me. It became easier, with practice, to focus on the life, love and laughter that I was able to share with Tom.

I still have occasions, where I Momentarily slip into self pity and grieving, but I ask Tom for his help and he is always there. I can feel his arms slide around me and a gentle kiss on the cheek. I can hear his gentle words, "I love you, Susie Q. I'm right here." And my world is right again.

Life is all about choices. We make 101 choices a day, whether with conscious intent or without. We make choices that make our life easier, and we also make choices that make our life more difficult.

Learning to be conscious of all our choices can be a challenging task. But if we make it a conscious choice to come from a place of abundance, then life can be much easier.

The Serenity Prayer comes to mind:

>God give me the serenity
>To accept the things, I cannot change
>The courage to change the things I can
>The wisdom to know the difference

Tom found this a difficult one on this side. He had a plateful of stressors, more than most of us. He struggled to deal with them; rise above them; understand them; cope with them. But it was a difficult process for him, as it is for many.

When we were talking about this chapter, he reminded me of a singer's story we listened to. She was a beautiful singer than had come from Ireland and had had some interesting experiences. She relayed a story where an arc angel, don't remember which one, sat at the foot of her bed and explained that if she could see the bigger picture, she would never be afraid.

Tom struggled to hold onto that story, but there were variables in his life that made it very difficult.

From the other side, he really pushes, come from a place of abundance, don't be afraid…

If only I could have integrated that (the lessons) on that side, life would have been so much easier. It is an important lesson to work at not only for the benefits of it over here, but for the benefits of it over there.

Chapter 20

Learning to Trust the Self

This chapter is a particularly powerful one for me. I went to a psychic years ago, who told me there were three types of people:

- Those who just existed
- Those who thought life was just a party
- Those who were here to learn

He stroked my ego by saying, that I was in the third group and he had never seen anyone work so hard at learning everything they could on every level of life. I remember when he said that, I thought, *"God, I wish that were really true."* BUT, he also said, "You have one last lesson that is going to be a challenge. The lesson is about trust."

I don't know about the ego stroking stuff, but he was right, I had a poor sense of trusting myself. I have gone through umpteen experiences, where if I had trusted myself instead of others, life would have been so much easier. I always tend to just give my trust away. I expect people to be honorable and to tell the truth; expect them to know what they are talking about; and expect them to follow through.

It doesn't take too much intelligence to figure out how many ways one can get "screwed" by living with those expectations. So, no need to expand on that.

Tom and I had both experienced challenging marriages. I think his was a lot worse than mine, but we both had reason not to want to get married again. Actually, for years we both declared that we would never get into a relationship again, which is one reason why we remained friends for so long.

Anyways, for the last several years, I have diligently worked on learning to NOT give my trust away AND learning to trust myself. Ha!

Tom and I worked on trust issues together and individually. We learned to trust each other with stuff we had never shared with anyone else before. That was pretty heavy duty in and of itself.

At one point on the other side, Tom said,

I always trusted you with everything. I trusted you more than I ever trusted anyone before. You were gifted and amazing. But also, because it was just you.

At another time, he said,

I was learning to love and trust in a way I had never done before. I learned to be open more than I ever had before. I was starting to be more aware and understand myself more than ever before. I was even trusting to talk with you about... despite feeling like a failure; and despite all the crap that came along with it. I trusted you. And I loved you. That was huge for me.

...

On the one hand, I spoke my truth more with you than with anyone. You knew more about all my vulnerabilities than anyone else... And I was learning to speak a truth that was both deeper and more real.

But then we also learned to trust ourselves and each other to get involved again. We had both wanted it for a long time. Actually, that part of our relationship is hilarious. Apart from the fact that we were both afraid of getting involved, we also both waited for the other to take the lead.

I was always taught that a lady always waits for the man to take the lead; and Tom had always thought a gentleman waits for a lady to take the lead. When we realized that that was part of what took us so long to get involved romantically, we had to laugh. But of course, those weren't the only reasons.

Trusting the self was a huge component. We both had to trust that we were "good enough" to be involved with someone. We had to trust both the self and one another. We both had our containers of fears to work through and we both didn't want to risk losing the friendship we had.

When Tom crossed over and we started a new kind of relationship, I had to trust myself that I wasn't going crazy. I had to trust that what I was feeling, then hearing, then seeing, was in fact Tom, and not just some figment of my imagination. That was a tough one for me. I wanted it so bad, but what if I was just creating it in my own mind?

What did make it all easier was that I had so many friends who believed that it was really happening; that there were so many other people that Tom was connecting with; but it was hard that his family wasn't interested and thought I was nuts.

But thanks predominantly to Tom, I was able to come through it all and learn to trust myself. It was kind of funny, I had the upmost trust in Tom; I just had to learn to trust me. And eventually I did. But it was a big lesson for me to learn.

Tom had already learned to trust himself. I had to laugh, "You beat me to it, My Love."

It was funny because we both trusted the other more than we trusted the self. When Tom finally decided to cross the bridge of friendship into romance, I had to ask, "Why and why now?"

His answer really threw me, "I just thought we were finally both ready."

Wow did that open a can of worms for conversation. And of course, one of the topics was all about trust. How he trusted me and knew that I trusted him.

Sometimes, it takes a lot of trust to grow and learn and move out of our comfort box; to expand our horizons; to move into fields of understanding whether socially, emotionally, psychologically, spiritually, in any aspect of life.

Tom says,

Its funny we come here to do that (to move past what we know into what we don't know with faith) and then we shut down or avoid the opportunities. Its too bad we don't take the curriculum with us, but then part of the curriculum is learning to trust without having a curriculum.

Knowing when to trust and when not to trust is a big part of that lesson. Both Tom and I had to learn to trust ourselves and to trust each other – much easier to do with the friendship than taking the risk of losing the friendship by crossing over that infamous bridge into romance.

But now I think back and think wow, I would have missed out on all of this if Tom hadn't been brave enough to cross that bridge.

Life really opens up when we let go of our fears and learn to trust.

Chapter 21

Givers and Takers

I have always seen people from the perspective of givers and takers. We all have the capacity for both, but what is more dominant in a given person helps to define a person.

From that we can determine that there are also three kinds of relationships:

- A taker and a taker
- A giver and a giver
- A taker and a giver

When you have two people who are both takers, it is going to be a challenging relationship. Who can 'out take' the other. If you both tend 'to take' in different areas of life, then it might work. But takers tend to take across the board.

If you have two givers, you are going to have a good relationship. They are both going to give and give. It is easier to work with these people. I always said that marriage should be a competition: who can make the other feel the most loved and special. This makes for a happy relationship when both partners are givers and try to make the other feel loved and special.

When you have both a taker and a giver – you end up with an abusive relationship.

Now the problem with all that, is that givers can also be martyrs and or controllers. That doesn't make for a good relationship. You have to be able to give and take in a healthy balance. When you give, it can make you feel like you are in control and often givers are passive controllers – you have to be careful.

If you keep giving at cost to the self and become a martyr, that doesn't work either.

However, when you are a giver, receiving can also make you feel vulnerable or not good enough, depending on what you are receiving and what your underlying life themes are about.

In a healthy relationship, you need to know how to give and take effectively and in balance. You give because you want to give, not to be in control but because you know what the other wants and you are happy to give it. You know when your partner needs you because you can both be open and honest about your needs.

You can also ask and receive without feeling less than or vulnerable.

Perhaps we need to be giving around 60% of the time and receiving about 40% of the time. If we are each working at that, I think we are doing pretty good.

The other aspect, of course, is taking the time to figure out what your partner actually needs and not just giving them what you want in return. They are not you and you are not them. We need to recognize that and learn to work with it.

One of the things that I thought was phenomenal about Tom on this side, especially coming from a male perspective, was that when I said something was important to me, or addressed something that I thought was unhealthy, his response was along the lines of: "Well, I never thought of that but if it is important to you, we will work on it." Or "Well, that's never been important to me, but if it's important to you, we will make it happen." Or, "I never thought of that, that sounds like a healthier relationship."

And he did work on it. And I thought that was awesome. Here is something he said about it on the other side:

You know I love you a lot. I will help you understand as we help you connect across the dimensions. But love is hugely important and all kinds of love. Well, no I don't think that is accurate. The infatuation kind of love isn't what it is all about. It is the deeper love that is about understanding and respect and acceptance. The kind of love where you give all you have and want to make the other person,... wrong word, you cannot make the other person happy, but where you want to learn what makes the other happy and willing to go out on a limb to support the other person with that.

When you told me things that were important to you, even if they were not important to me, I went out of my way to make them happen for you because it was important to you and I loved you. It is about giving without being a martyr. It is about supporting without enabling. It is about respect and consideration and cooperation and all the things that you taught me about.

But it is way more than that. It is also about allowing and accepting the others' thoughts, feelings, beliefs, even when they are not yours. Like you did with me about Wreck Beach. I loved the sense of freedom with it and you did not criticize me or negate me even though you didn't agree with me. You simply accepted it and allowed it to be me...you knew about my issues and accepted me regardless.

When I asked for help you always gave what you could. When I didn't understand you clarified without negation. That was loving.

You did a beautiful job of it. I didn't. I was scared. It would come through at times and you would just hold it. You didn't demand anything, you just gave. Well except for when it came to time management. I gave by trying to do anything I could for you. With the house. With the car. With being supportive and understanding.

With me it was more about behavior. With you it was more about the psychological aspects if you want. We both did what we could and when we messed up, we worked through it and found different ways of operating. You were much better at that than me. But I was willing to listen and understand and work with it.

Ultimately, I just had a lot more crap on my plate and I apologize for that. And the fact that I was learning how much crap I had on my plate reinforced that I wasn't good enough...one of my life long issues. But I hope you understand how much I did and do love you.

I have seen your thoughts about Cozumel. When I said to you, "You know how much I love you." And your thought was "No I don't. I don't have a clue." But you didn't say anything.

I understand, and I guess it is both too bad that you didn't question me, and it is also too bad that I didn't know enough to clarify. But it did scare me how much I loved you and how vulnerable I was with you. I often said things to you and expected you to criticize me or come down on me in some way...and you wouldn't say anything. You would just let it be...why?

As always, I loved it when Tom just talked, and I could just listen and type out what he said, but at this point he was asking, and I had no idea how to answer.

Can you give me an example?

You already heard the example I was thinking of...that time when we were driving, and I explained how difficult the time management thing was for me. You never said anything. I was at a loss. I didn't know if I had done something good or bad. Eventually you said, "Thank you for that." but that was all.

Time management was a big issue for me. I always tried to respect other people's time and hate it when people have no respect for my time. Due to physical pain and marital issues, Tom learned to never plan anything in advance. Whereas for me to be as productive as I am, I learned to organize my time. I had no problem making Tom a priority, but I needed to know when in advance, so that I could organize my day around him. It was regularly an issue between us.

I was always pushing Tom to identify what he wanted or needed from me or what he didn't like. He had a difficult time doing that. But on this one occasion, while we were driving, he said he knew that I was always asking him to identify any issue and so he would address this one. It was hard for him. He went on and on about how he understood how important it was to me; how I organized my time effectively to be as productive as I was; that I did more than anyone else he knew, etc., but that he had a difficult time organizing time in advance. It didn't come easy. He explained how sorry he was that it frustrated me and that he was really working at it. When he finished, I didn't say anything. I just let him sit with the fact that he could acknowledge something and there was no backlash.

So, at this point, with him on the other side, I explained,

I wanted you to just be okay with explaining how and why it was frustrating for you. I didn't want to give you anything positive or negative. It was about you. Not about me. I knew what you would have got from your ex if you had shared something like that with her and I wanted it to be an experience that you created for yourself, without my input.

Well I guess that reflected the fears I had. On the one hand, I was afraid I would get something from you like from my ex...but on the other hand, I trusted you that it would be safe. It was a double-edged sword. I actually thought you would or maybe I wanted you to tell me I did a good job. Hmmm. That's interesting. I was looking for your validation and you made me give it to myself. I just got it. Thank you for that. And I did give it to myself.

When you wouldn't give me what I wanted, I did tell myself I did a good job. Wow...it's taken till now to figure that out. Again, thank you.

My pleasure my Jedi Master – glad I could be of service...ha ha.

(I explained earlier that Tom's brother started the joke about Tom being a Jedi Master, and it stuck.)

Tom said a lot in this narrative. He was able to acknowledge and validate, for himself, that he did listen and attempted to do what I asked for in the relationship. That we need to give without being a martyr. He acknowledged a number of different aspects of loving someone. I thought what he said was great.

He acknowledged how important it is for us to allow each other to have our own perspectives and opinions without judgement or criticism. He acknowledged that it is important to accept and to give without criticism or negation. I particularly loved that he acknowledged that he wanted me to give him the validation but when I didn't, he gave it to himself. That was a huge step for Tom.

He was able to acknowledge how much he gave and on how many levels. That we both gave in the ways that we knew how.

I love it when Tom just starts talking, I could just sit and listen to him all day. But this was a beautiful "passage" if you will, about what a good healthy relationship can be about. I loved it.

Another interesting aspect is that when Tom walked through the experience on the other side, he actually did some learning. He became aware of a process and just through recall of an experience, gained a level of learning. So again, what we do on this side, helps to prepare us for what we can do on the other side.

Chapter 22

Moving Between Dimensions

Historically, I understood the dimensions from an old Christian polarized perspective, heaven and hell. That is, an "All or None" perspective. All/None," "Black/White", "Us/Them" perspectives are considered to be intellectually and psychologically immature. This kind of childlike thinking causes a lot of dissention in the world.

By the time I was 12 years old, I had read the Bible 10 times. The Old Testament was a difficult reading because Numbers was so boring. So eventually, I started at the end of the Old Testament and went backwards through the books. And I did it.

Along the way, the Pastor of our church was incredibly patient with all the questions I had. Why was the Bible so contradictory was a primary concern? I brought 42 contradictions, in the New Testament alone, to him. One of the big issues I had was that the Bible indicated that John the Baptist was the reincarnation of Elijah, yet the "Church" claimed reincarnation was wrong.

Then I studied what happened at the Table of Constantinople and discovered the distorted evolution of Christianity and how it continued to get more distorted throughout the centuries. And of course, I had to challenge him with that too.

The pastor tried hard to answer my questions. But I rarely got answers that I was satisfied with. There were just too many times, he didn't have answers for the questions I asked. Poor guy.

One day he phoned my Mom and asked what we talked about at the dinner table. My Mom was rather taken back and questioned him about why he was asking. He said because he had a congregation of over 600 and no one brought him the questions that I did. My Mom apparently just laughed, and told him she was glad it was him I was asking, and not her.

Then at the age of 14, I read Edgar Cayce's biography, There Is a River which expanded my understanding of the dimensions. In Cayce's readings, he claimed that we are spiritual beings having a material experience giving us opportunities to learn and develop spiritual awareness so that we can eventually move back to the One. The experiences we chose to create here can turn into positives or negatives depending on how we deal with them. In the various Cayce books, he talks at length about the different dimensions. I loved it.

At 18, I read Autobiography of a Yogi. I loved what Yogananda's mentor, Sri Yukteswar, claimed. He claimed that there are three main divisions of experience: the material, the astral and the causal. That we move back and forth between the material and the astral planes until we learn all that we need to. Then we move on, going back and forth between the astral and the causal planes until we finish with the astral. When we finish with the causal plane, we return to the One or Source or God or whatever you want to call it.

As I started to research and understand the different religions from around the world, I was given the opportunity to create a curriculum on World Religions. It was an awesome opportunity and I found it fascinating.

Then I wanted to study astrophysics and understand how it all worked together, but I got sidetracked in university and came out a psychologist. Oh well. Don't worry, after practicing with the limitations of psychology for twenty years, I moved on. Actually, for the last ten years I practiced as a psychologist, I was enrolled in other programs, designations and degrees, so that I could help people grow and learn and heal more effectively.

In today's world, the internet is inundated with information through channelers, psychics and others regarding various issues from Ascension, to multiple Dimensions, to visitations and interactions with various energy forms or beings throughout the universe.

Tom was very interested in all of this. He also read the Cayce books; <u>Autobiography of a Yogi</u>; anything on ascension and the after life. He got into Dr Steven

Greer's work; and regularly listened to a variety of different channelings on YouTube; he listened to various types of meditations that focused on developing the higher self and much more. He wanted more out of life. He wanted to believe that there was more to this life than what we experienced. He wanted to move through ascension and go into the different dimensions. The more he learned, the more he wanted. I loved it.

I approached it a little differently than Tom. I believed that we choose to come to this plane for a reason and I wanted to live this life to the fullest; experience everything I needed to experience to learn, resolve, let go or whatever, so that I didn't have to come back.

And now, Tom is in a different dimension, apparently learning how to move through even more dimensions using different types of portals. He works with different ways to raise or alter his vibrational frequency so that he can maneuver through the portals.

Leaving me here, struggling to figure out how to learn from him on the other side. I use the word "struggle" because it has been a challenging road to learn how to connect with him.

Tom's underlying life theme and driving force on this side were about fun and adventure. He has taken those personality characteristics with him to the other side and continues to explore and understand the various dimensions of life with fun.

Early on, in our newly developing connection, Terry explained,

- *Tom will help you with the automatic writing, but he will also help you move between dimensions with intent*
- *He will also help you to see him*
- *You will need to work at keeping balance between the different dimensions – ALL WORLDS*
- *You will work with 3-4-5th dimensions and moving in and out of space*
- *Remember to keep it all balanced*

At another time, she said:

- *Tom will teach you to travel across space and time and other dimensions*
- *He will teach you to go across different realms with intent*

Wow! I would move between dimensions. That sounded really cool. But how was Tom going to teach me?

At the point of writing this book, I haven't yet learned to do that. I have had some pretty weird experiences, but I don't think I have crossed any dimensions at this point. On the other hand, I have had some interesting OBE and astral travel experiences and gone through some weird portals.

I am interjecting at this point with the final edit. I have now apparently crossed over four times. The first three times, I had no recall other than it was a really weird experience. Very different from meditation or sleep or a seizure. The first two times and the fourth time was when I was in meditation with friends and the third, I was meditating on my own. The first three times there was an awareness that something very different had happened, but I had no recall of it. It was almost like having a petite mal seizure. There was just a blank. But this kind of blank space was different in that there was an awareness that something had definitely happened. I just didn't know what it was.

When I asked Tom what happened, he said,

Way to go. You just crossed over. I know you don't remember what happened, but that isn't important right now. What is important is that you crossed over, the rest will come.

Wow! Really? I talked about it with the friends I was meditating with and what they had experienced.

The second time, Tom started dancing with me in celebration before the meditation was finished. That was great in and of itself. We were dancing in the energetic field. My body was sitting on the chair. As much as I want to learn how to cross over, dancing with Tom was more important in the Moment.

The fourth time was even more amazing. I was aware of moving into this phenomenal light. I understand why people call it a "white light", but I wouldn't have called it a "white light". But it was full. I think I would say I "felt" the light more than "saw" the light and yet it was all around me. I was so "full" of "love" as I sat in the chair. It was hard for me to explain what had just happened to my friends. Tom was so excited, he was just beaming. I was so excited and can't wait to see what happens next.

In the meantime, back to this book that I am editing…

I am also waiting for Tom to come back through a portal into this dimension.

Tom and I had the following discussion one morning:

Well I think you are on a new journey. We are moving together in an area we are both familiar with from this lifetime but never had an actual experience of. We prepared for it well, both in this lifetime and in prior lifetimes. We need to get rid of any old layers of beliefs, hurts, programs, etc. so that we can indeed move forward. Yeah, I think it is a good reflection of what is going on…I remember us discussing your dreams about ascension.

Hold on a minute, I need to go back and remember. Yes, I remember I was upset with you because you went on ahead of me. You said you needed to prepare some things before I could come across and I was supposed to stay here to help others. Wow! I totally forgot about those dreams. There were a whole series of them. I remember one of the farmhouses I was in. You came back (across the dimensions) to help me, and we were trying to figure out how you came across. We were working on figuring out how to go back and forth across the "veil". Holy cow! That is so like what is going on now...we need to meditate on this and see if we are on the right track. Thank you for reminding me.

Wow...just wow...

Yes, I think we are on track. We just need to get you meditating more and deeper and we will achieve it all. You always wanted it all...we will make this happen...this is exciting...

Was the series of dreams indicative of or a premonition of what is going on now? The dreams were a few years prior, but they sure seemed to parallel what was currently happening.

In one of the dreams, the one I mentioned in the dialogue, I was in an old farmhouse. I came around from the kitchen into a hallway and Tom came through the door at the end of the hallway. We were both so excited. We just held each other for the longest time. Then we tried to figure out how he did it. He didn't know how.

In another dream, we figured out how he came across and we started going back and forth between the dimensions with intent. We spoke at length and decided it was better if I stayed and worked with people here. I was to help them heal and prepare for ascension. Tom would stay on the other side and help people cross over. But we could now "travel" back and forth across the dimensions easily, to be with one another.

I would love it if Tom could learn how to move through the portal to come back here. While waiting for the new house to be completed, I am staying at a friend's place – an old farmhouse. At one end of the hallway is the kitchen and at the other end is my bedroom door. Every time I come around the kitchen into the hallway, I am expecting Tom to come through that doorway. Being the romantic I am, I especially focus on it with every one of our original anniversaries and again with each of our current anniversaries; and on our birthdays; okay, so any time that it might be a special occasion. But alas, I am still waiting and expecting.

Not sure how physical or material his body would be, but at least I could see him then. And if we could learn how to move back and forth, that would be the ultimate. Well at least for me, at this point in time. I would think that once we achieved that, there would probably be something else we would start working on to achieve.

All I can say is I am doing the work Tom tells me to do and I have learned to do the OBEs and astral travel. Who knows what is yet to come.

Chapter 23

Awareness

This chapter makes me laugh, for a number of reasons. First, in psychology we are always attempting to increase one's awareness: what are your underlying life themes; your value systems; how you interpret the world; your reactions to those interpretations; how and why you developed the programs and filters you have; etc. etc.

But when I did my Ayurveda internships in India, I was fascinated by how they all laughed at Western psychology and thought we didn't have a clue about consciousness and awareness. In the West, we were still in kindergarten! Oh dear.

So of course, I wanted to know more. I found it to be a fascinating subject and yes, the Western perspective has a long way to go.

Then Tom crosses over and we have all these dialogues about learning and consciousness and awareness.

In the chapter on learning, Tom talks about how learning is about developing awareness. But in this chapter, Tom wanted to explore awareness in an entirely different way.

When you start developing awareness of other subtler energies, you start to become aware of movement in an entirely different way. Like when Katherine was aware of Tom's movement around me. Or when Rudy was aware of Tom's movement in the restaurant (See Chapter 33.).

Awareness in meditation also deepens. Or at least it did for me.

Think of a wine connoisseur. If you haven't tasted wine before, and you are at a wine tasting, you would probably be able to differentiate some basic crude differences, for instance how dry or sweet it is. But the more you work at identifying the differing subtler components, the better you get at identifying whether is has been corked, or the bouquet, acidity, balance, body, complexity, crispness, the aeration or finish of the wine.

The same parameters occur with energy. The more you work at differentiating the subtler energies, whether you have terminology for the differences or not, the more aware you become of them: in or around the body; fast or slow; heaviness or lightness; the vibrational frequency; denseness/thickness or clarity; etc.

I would expect that this style of awareness applies to a vast number of issues in life. It is interesting when it applies to the unseen world. Those who have no interest or who are bound by limiting beliefs would not explore the subtler aspects and work with these concepts. But the more open minded, interested people will know exactly what I am talking about.

For Tom, awareness is key. You can love without awareness of these deeper aspects. But can you have this kind of awareness and not love at a deeper level?

Tom suggested that love is like water. He suggested that gratitude and appreciation might be compared to the hydrogen and oxygen molecules while awareness might be like the hydrogen bonds that connect the hydrogen and oxygen and the H_2O molecules that make up water.

Interesting analogy. Who would have thought to compare love to water?

Let's not forget that water has 63 anomalies that we still don't understand. Kind of like the many layers of love.

This analogy brings up concepts concerning water and consciousness and intent presented by Dr. Emoto.

I will let you play with it.

Chapter 24

Dying, Death and Dead

I really don't like these words. Yes, I understand that they are meant to convey what has happened to the physical body on this side, but they are such limiting words that distort what is really going on.

It really hit me one day, when I heard my Dad explain to a friend that "both Mom and Tom died". By that time, we had both seen Tom and I constantly heard and felt him, he didn't die! He was very much alive, just in a different dimension.

People or souls or whatever you want to call them at that point, move across the 'great divide', but are still very much alive. And in fact, one might argue that they are more alive on the other side than we are here. They have greater awareness and don't have, or at least have the opportunity to release, all the limiting beliefs, fears and programs they developed on this side. We could argue that it is our limiting beliefs, fears and programs that make us "more dead" than they, if you will.

You may laugh at the term, "more dead" ("Word" doesn't like this term) or "deader" but with what science is now learning, it might be a more appropriate term. The body can still function in a variety of diverse ways, once the "energy", that many people think of as the "soul", has left the body. Suffice it to say, I think the "personality energy" has left the body, but the "soul" is at a much deeper level yet. But that is a whole other issue that we won't get into here.

For the longest time, I have believed that people will experience, whatever they believe will happen, when they first cross over. Until they are grounded, so to speak, and are ready to experience all that there is to experience, they probably just experience what they expect to experience. Tom certainly reinforces that belief, but he also adds to it.

For instance, Tom claims that he and my Mom have gone through entirely different processes or journeys on the other side. We had the following conversation at one point in time,

Dad asked me to ask you about my Mom? Do you connect with her or see her or anything?

No, she is on her own journey, but she appears to be in a healing process...not sure what her stuff is about.

And then at another time,

Have you seen Mom? Does she know it's her birthday on this side?

Yes, she said she doesn't know how to connect yet. So, she asked me to send a big hug to your Dad. She says to thank you for being there with him. And she sends her love to both of you. She wasn't clear when I saw her, it

was like her energy blended in and out. So, I don't know if there was more. That was all I got.

Why is her energy blending in and out?

I think it's just because we are operating differently. In different spectrums or dimensions or frequencies or something. Don't need to worry, there is nothing wrong with her it's just like we are on two different waves. So, it makes it hard to connect.

But I think she is very much aware of the connection that you and I have. So, she knew I could convey the message for her. She has a very pretty energy. It's not at all like my Mom's, but it is still very beautiful. I think she is working on her own healing – like it is the solar plexus – if we were looking at the chakras...it comes through that it has to do with the 6 & 7 DNA levels...

Ok so, 6 is about communication balance and harmony and 7 is about spiritual awareness and development, according to what I have – is that what you think as well.

Well that is sort of it. But it is more than that...you have to take into consideration of the fact that they are all very interactive and inter-dynamic as well as what is dominant on either side...but that is the primary gist of it.

So, going back to the beginning of the chapter, to use words like dying, death and dead, just seems so inappropriate. For me, at least, those words have a real finality about them. And, of course, there is no finality.

From a biochemistry perspective, the first laws have to do with not being able to create or eliminate energy, energy simply transforms.

Well, that is what we do. We transform if you will. We lose the physical, material, Newtonian, chemical aspect of our beingness and move on with the energetic aspect. But that is just a personal belief. Should ask Tom about that one day, along with the 10,000 other questions I am always asking.

In most religions there is a belief of an afterlife. Christians believe we go to heaven or hell, a very polarized belief. Most of the world believes in some form of reincarnation – and there are a lot of different versions of reincarnation. So, in my mind, the question really isn't about whether they are alive, but rather what does their "alive" consist of.

Another aspect of this we might want to entertain is that according to Western biology, "life" is defined as anything that is carbon based. Personally, I think that definition reflects incredibly immature thinking and simple mindedness. Why can't life be based on another element or electro-magnetic based or another vibrational frequency or anything else. Believing that life has to be carbon based is as naïve and egocentric as believing that we are the only intelligent beings in the universe. But those are just my beliefs.

Anyways, Tom is definitely not dead, he is very much alive. He is full of love and laughter and fun and let's not forget adventure. He continues to have a great personality and an inquisitive mind. He is loving and affectionate, considerate and a beautiful being.

He certainly wasn't perfect while he was on this side, and I assume that he isn't perfect on the other side. We are all on our own journey of growth and healing and learning or awareness. I would think when we meet perfection, we simply blend into the oneness. Or maybe we start all over again with another journey. I have no idea and nor does Tom, at this point.

The bottom line is: He is very much alive!

The physical body stopped functioning, but we can also say that the energy of the physical body started to transform into other energies: He most certainly isn't dead.

When we start to really grasp that it is just a change in energy. When we begin to appreciate that when we cross over, we are simply in different dimensions, it should help us deal with "losing" a loved one. Although, I admit, it doesn't entirely solve or eliminate grieving. It just makes it easier.

I give Tom a bad time, that he makes it difficult to grieve him when he is always there. But, I still go through bouts of tears and grieving, when I really want him on this side of the "veil" with me, physically.

So, I have to remind myself to come from a place of abundance and not a place of lack.

I also have the phenomenal opportunity of asking Tom to help me and he is always there, putting his arm around me and letting me know how much he loves me and that we will be together in the same dimension, soon. But he also reminds me that I have still a lot of work to do.

So, I laugh and tell him, "Not soon enough".

But if we could all be more open to "allowing" those who cross over to "connect" with us, I think it would benefit us greatly as we go through our "grieving process" or maybe we should call it our "transformation process". We are transforming: how we connect; how we communicate; and how we relate to one another.

I think it is a lot more difficult to deal with grieving if we focus on death and dead, i.e., a dead-end road, as opposed to transition, i.e., a continuing road.

From Tom's perspective, he laughs and says,

I am a lot more alive over here than I was over there, and I have a lot more love to give from this side.

Chapter 25

Energies, Frequencies and Vibrations

I am not sure if Tom knew who Nikola Tesla was, I don't remember talking about Tesla with Tom. But Tom's name for the chapter is interesting. Remember what Tesla said, "If you want to find the secrets of the universe, think in terms of energy, frequency and vibration."

Energy. That is such a hugely diverse word. It is almost as bad as "love" in terms of what it might mean. We use it to convey:

- mechanical energy
- chemical energy
- kinesthetic energy
- potential energy
- electrical energy
- atomic energy
- light energy
- sound energy
- quantum energy
- etc.

So, what are we really saying? A simple explanation might be, 'that which is without physical form as we understand it now'.

On this side, Tom and I did talk a lot about frequencies and vibrations. Although doing the research Tom keeps sending me to do now, I think maybe we had a very distorted understanding of it.

From a scientific perspective, frequency is the cyclic pattern of scalar waves that flash on and off, while the vibrational frequency is the rate at which energy units contract and expand. Tom and I certainly never discussed energy in that manner before.

When we talked about vibrations and frequencies, we were referring to the motion going on in the body; or how fast I could feel the energy moving or vibrating in my body. We both laughed that if we could get the vibration going fast enough, we might be able to move through a portal into another dimension.

There is also the energy mechanics definition – when energy contracts it is a vibration; when it expands it is an oscillation; and the combination is the vibrational frequency. Nope, we didn't discuss it this way either.

If we look at energy in terms of light, then we look at the light creating flashing patterns; scalar waves operate like on/off switches and are called partiki phasing. The speed at which partiki expands/contracts or turns off/on is the frequency of the scalar waves. The phasing of these energy patterns is believed to be processed by our consciousness and our DNA before we even come into the material reality. The possibility of patterns in infinite.

From this perspective, it is the interaction between the flashing patterns of energy, and the electromagnetic fields of sound and light, that allow us to come into existence.

Frequency and sound are supposedly the basics of sacred geometry.

Some frequencies are harmful to the body, i.e.., various electromagnetic frequencies generated from wireless products. Those frequencies can disrupt the natural flow and or rhythm innate to the body: the body systems, organs, cells and organelles; and over time can cause health issues.

On the other hand, there are various energies that resonate and support the natural rhythms of the body.

Rife's work back in the 1920s identified various frequencies in the body and utilized specific frequencies to eliminate disease.

Some people believe that eating various foods can also disrupt the natural rhythms. Certainly, most agree that many foods in today's world are full of toxins and depleted in nutrients and as a result have a negative impact on body functions.

Bruce Tainio of Tainio Technology designed a monitor to ascertain different frequencies in the human body. The brain's frequency runs about 72MHz while the body ran between 62-78 MHz. He claimed that when the body went down to 60 or below, the immune system had a difficult time functioning.

He also identified that junk food ran at 0 Hz and thus was not helpful. Whereas, he felt that the frequency that the body needed to have that was at least at a frequency of 60 MHz.

(http://energyfanatics.com/2014/06/04/what-is-frequency-how-energy-wave-affects-your-wellbeing/

http://www.bodymaintenance101.com/keep-your-bodys-healing-frequency-high/

http://www.qrg.northwestern.edu/projects/vss/docs/Communications/1-what-is-frequency.html)

So back to Tom. He claims that when we raise our vibrational frequency, we can move through portals. Which of course, provokes more questions...

    1) How do we raise our vibrational frequency?
    2) What are portals?

Chapter 26

Portals

Geez, I thought I understood what Tom meant by portals, but now I am really confused. Maybe in writing this chapter with him, I will get if figured out. I'm hoping.

First off, I thought when he talked of portals, there was one type of portal – NOPE! I thought portals were gateways to other dimensions. Well some are, but others aren't! Oh dear!

Apparently emotional portals help connect our Chakras to our Twelve Layers of DNA. They are very different than other kinds of portals and I am thinking that there are even more kinds of portals. But currently, that is all I am hearing about. The emotional portals are discussed more in, Tom: Cosmic Healing.

So, in order to move through different dimensions, we need to raise our vibrational frequencies, which may mean the speed at which scalar waves moves, or maybe that is just how we see it in our 3-Dimensional minds.

I can say from personal experience, that when I was working with the Merkaba at one point, it scared me because it was moving so fast. It felt out of control. I wish I could have stayed with it, if that is what is required to cross dimensions. I haven't got there again, yet. (Although that changed by the time of this book's last edit.)

Maybe that is why Tom and I both loved speed. When we took a 6,500 km ground trip, he averaged at 170 kmh and I averaged 160 kmh. We both like speed! We also both love roller coasters and other types of rides, although neither of us like rides that go around in circles, it makes us both sick. There might be a symbolism in all of that…we like to go fast, but we like to move forward, as opposed to going in circles. Hmmm.

Anyways, another component of the portals is that we need to let go of fear in order to go through them. Fear obviously had an impact when I got going fast with the Merkaba. So, I have to work with that. Funny, I grew up with my father saying, "She's not smart enough to be afraid". He always thought I took way too many risks because I liked speed and adventure and he didn't.

I usually confront fear head on and push through it. For instance, with my fear of heights, I learned how to sky dive. On the other hand, I would never take an entertainment drug. I never even smoked or drank alcohol or coffee. They didn't make sense to me. But Tom was on the opposite end of the continuum when it came to those kinds of experiences.

Tom's issues with fear were more about fear of rejection and not being good enough, as opposed to fear with anything adventurous. So, if he got going that fast, he would probably think it was a blast.

When I asked Terry about the portals, she said,

- *Discover, embrace, manifest:*
- *Tom says, "Do it with your mind, you have it all right there"*
- *Don't be so analytical and let Tom show you the way*
- *Let go of body, mind, spirit*
- *There are three levels:*
  1. *emotional that link chakra with DNA*
  2. *dimensional – obviously move through different dimensions*
  3. *sacred geometry and the Merkaba: as you work on it, you will create an added step to the self evolution thru the Merkaba*

When I asked Terry about the Merkaba and how to use it, she said she didn't know. She didn't really understand the Merkaba and so couldn't be of any help.

Bottom line? There are a variety of different types of portals to go through. They require that we drop the fear and move through them. Whether the fears be about psychological issues, i.e., fear of rejection; or whether they are about physiological issues, i.e.., fear of speed; fears block our capacity to go through portals.

Chapter 27

Can One Soul Occupy Two Bodies Simultaneously

This Chapter wasn't in the original book. I didn't know how to deal with it, so I left it out. But then...

Let's start at the beginning, so to speak. When I taught world religions, years ago...we won't say how long ago that was...I learned that several African and the major Australian aboriginals believed that one soul could occupy more than one body at the same time, thus allowing the self to challenge or provoke the self to learn and grow. Interesting concept.

Anyways, because a good friend, GG, is so much like Tom, I questioned Tom as to whether one soul could occupy more than one body. Tom said yes. Interesting.

Next time I saw Terry an interesting thing happened. I asked Terry the same question. A puzzled look came over her face and she said.

- *I don't know. I am getting a definite yes from Tom but my guide, (Tony) said no. I have no idea why or what to do with that.*

In my mind, ever the skeptic, I thought, hmmm, is she just covering her butt? She has told me so many things that she couldn't possibly know, but this seems a little weird.

I didn't know what to with it, so I decided to leave it out of the book.

But…while doing the final editing on the book, another friend who really liked Tom, Colin, phoned. After talking about a few other things, Colin says, "Holly, I have been meaning to ask you this for ages, but I was really pushed to phone and ask this morning…"

Really pushed? Hmmm.

Anyways, he continued, I remember you making a comment about Tom a while back and you were asking, and I want to know what the answer was…Can a soul occupy two bodies at the same time?"

Interesting question from out of the blue, don't you think?

Tom pushed and said, "Maria's book." That was it, nothing more.

Let's take a little diversion and I will explain. Maria's book is one of the books from my Entwined Collection. It was written when I was on holidays, a few years back, down in the Dominican Republic. When I started to write the book, I had a given format and process in mind. It didn't work that way at all! The writing was "driven". I had never had an experience like that before. The book turned out incredibly different than I had intended. The book was written in a very scattered manner. I normally write in a very linear sequential manner. There were concepts in the book, I had never thought of before. It was an amazing experience. I shared the experience with a few friends when I came home, and repeatedly it was suggested that, "The book was channelled."

Well okay, interesting concept but I wasn't aware of anyone being there to do the channeling. But whatever.

I was waiting to get the book covers for the Entwined Collection done professionally before I published them. I wanted a consistent theme for all the books as each book was "written" by a character in the first book. That whole process got put on hold when Tom and my Mom decided to cross over.

The covers for Tom's Collection and the Entwined Collection are now finished. So, I started doing the final edits on the books. I finished the last edit of the Dominican book, Maria's book, A <u>Love that Crosses Time</u>, a few weeks ago.

It was an amazing book to reread. So much of it I hadn't remembered writing. Over the past few years, I occasionally thought of the book and thought I should expand on given parts. They were already done. Likewise, parts that I thought I needed to condense – were already done. I didn't even remember many parts that I had written.

When I got to page 25, I stopped editing the book, grabbed a cup of tea and just sat and read the book. It was fascinating. AND, so much of it that was Tom and I both on this side as well as, on both sides of the veil. Yet, was written before we ever became romantic! Rereading it was an amazing experience that repeatedly sent goose bumps up and down my arms.

I shared the new experience with several friends saying my life is just getting more and more weird!

Anyways, back to Colin and his question. The answer was in Maria's book, A Love that Crosses Time! Which is why Tom simply said, "Maria's Book". AND, the book even explained how both Terry's guide and Tom were right! Wow!

When I explained all that to Colin, Tom said, "Now put that in the book!" So yes, a soul can occupy different bodies at the same time. Apparently, it all depends on an interaction between your awareness and your vibrational frequency and how you choose to function.

Chapter 28

When You Ask, Wait for the Answers

This lesson is kind of funny and really takes me to task. As a therapist I can have the "patience of Job". I will take you to task and hold you accountable, but I will be patient with you while you are in the learning process.

When it comes to me and my private life, I have no patience at all. I want it all and I want it yesterday, and I hate the learning curve – which Tom always laughed at.

Well, I apparently didn't have much patience with Tom on the other side. If I didn't get answers right away, I moved on. I figured it was my issue and I wasn't doing something right. So, I was taken to task.

The second time I saw Terry, it was in another group demonstration program and she pointed me out in the group and said,

- *You are asking the right questions*
- *He is talking with you, but you don't give him enough time to answer*
- *You need to take more time to listen*
- *You need to be more patient*

- *Your mind gets up and moves on before you are able to receive the answer*
- *But he is trying to give you the answers*
- *You need to be patient..."*

Suzanna was with me at that presentation as well, and she just started chuckling, "Yup, that's Holly, she wants it all yesterday. Doesn't give herself the time of day."

And she was right. I expected Tom to come through right away. When I did start hearing him, it was difficult. It was hard to hear him, and I had to really focus. But if I could at least hear something, then I would stay and focus and work with it. When I heard nothing, I just walked away and shrugged my shoulders, with an "oh well" attitude.

I am sure with people like Terry and Mary who had this gift from childhood, it was easy to know and understand when you needed to wait for the answers. But for a novice like me, I had to learn.

So, if you are wanting to engage in the process or you are working through the learning curve, be patient and wait for the answers. Eventually they will come faster and faster.

And don't forget, they may not always be what you want to hear. Or go where you expect to go.

Chapter 29

What is Love

A universal question that has been asked through the ages. Historically, when Tom and I discussed love, it was in terms of the six different types of love identified in old Greek culture and philosophy.

We agreed that we had the type of love between good friends. We often talked how it was deeper than most friendships and why it was so different.

Then when we became partners, we discussed what love meant to us on that level. The first time Tom told me he loved me, he was drunk. I had purposefully got him drunk on a holiday. I had known Tom for years and known that he used to be a big drinker. But he rarely drank in front of me and our friends, only when he was out with the boys. So, I wanted to know what he was like when he had too much. Well, he was an absolute hoot. I don't think I have ever laughed so hard. I always told him I would tease him "to his dying day" about his antics that day. Now I think that is hilarious because I still tease him. But then, in terms of the previous chapter, he hasn't 'died'.

But that was also the first time he told me how much he loved me as a partner, as opposed to as a friend. So, in my mind it didn't count.

The next time he told me loved me, I had to "pull a Holly". I asked him what that meant for him. He gave the most perfect answer:

- *I love how you make me feel about me*
- *I love who you are*
- *And I love how we are together*

Being the romantic that I am, that was such a beautiful answer. And he was a guy!!

So now that he was on the other side, I wanted to know what love meant for him over there. I got a number of answers. I will go over what some of the psychics and mediums have said, and then will explore some of Tom's comments.

First, remember my story about the psychic Jane, who Tom and I went to when we were still just friends? During that session, she said,

- *Well you have a strong partnership now – an unusually close friendship energy – strong intimacy – like a couple*

Then later in the session, she said.

- *If he was on his death bed – he would tell you, you were his true love*
- *There is a strong love and warmth an authentic love between you"*

Then when I phoned Jane after Tom had crossed over, she said,

- *The two of you had a very strong love...*
- *The love between you is still very much there and is still strong*

Then the next psychic I saw, Mary, said,

- *He really loves you*

Later in the session,

- *Your love will grow stronger*
- *He keeps saying how much he loves you and he is there with you*
- *The more you believe and trust in him, the stronger your relationship will get*

Near the end, she said,

- *He keeps sending you so much love, you need to know how much he loved you"*

Then we have "Messages from the Other Side'

- *Your husband is coming in strong; ...he really loves you... like he really loves you*

Then later,

- *He really loves you a lot"*

And again at the end,

- *Again, he really does love you*

- *It's important to understand how much he loves you*

Then from the Channeler we got

- *She is my bright "light"*
- *She is my true love*
- *She is my helper*

Then from Terry I got,

- *His attention to you is particularly important because you both want to be together*

Later in the session,

- *He didn't express how much he really cared for you when here; how much he really loved you; he told you that he loved you, but couldn't express the depth of it, there was a lot of fear around it*

Later in that session,

- *Again, he says he couldn't express how much he loved you. It was part of his human lesson. He carried a tremendous amount of fear. The fear stopped him in so many ways.*

And another time,

- *He says that love means different things between different people and his love for you is authentic."*

And at another time, when I asked Terry what love means to him now, she responded.

- *More passionate*
- *More deeper*

- *More understanding*
- *Less physical*
- *More universal*
- *He showed Terry himself standing on a mountain top and she said:*
- *Everything was brighter... the grass greener... the sky bluer...*
- *From where he is love is much brighter and much deeper*
- *He connects with you and you trust him with it*
- *And he is so much more enlightened now*

Then from Mary, the second time, I got,

- *He's very upset at leaving you*
- *He loved you very much*

Later in the session when I asked what love meant to him on the other side,

- *Eternal love*
- *His love is very powerful – but he's not able to send all of it right now*
- *It is a very powerful force*
- *The love he has for you – its everything; nothing is left out of it; it is all; nothing is left out*
- *Its heart, soul & spirit – its everything – there is nothing missing*

- *There are all different kinds of love – but his is "all encompassing"*

But for me, Tom's words of love are much more powerful. We have talked a lot about love. Here are a few of his comments:

You saved me on that side, I've told you that before. ...on so many occasions. You were my source of love on that side, but you are on this side too. But its more on this side and there is so much love all around here. It is easy to love from here. There aren't all the fears and the inadequacies that get in the way. And I am surrounded by love, so it is easier to love you. There is just so much.

It's like on that side I could only connect with you so far...on this side it just goes so much further. See I can see it or feel it when you fill up with love and gratitude like that. I could only sense that to a minor degree on that side. On this side, I feel it, sense it and be with it, like I can breathe it right into me. I wish I could explain it better.

Just know that I love you far more than you can possibly understand on that side. That we go back a long way. That we have a mutual ongoing purpose and we will get there.

I was told I could be of more help to you on this side than on that side. It was a fundamental choice. To be of greater good here or of less good over there. Our love was strong enough to handle it. There was no harm or judgement in the choice. It was just a fundamental choice of where I could be of the most good and reach my higher potential.

You really need to know how much...it transcends time and space...our love really is deep ... it is profound as many have said...it's funny because as much as I think you were able to express your love more than I was...I think I am the one who was more aware of how deep it was...maybe that is part of what scared me so much. That is why I was so afraid to lose you. I just didn't believe I was worthy of it and it was so much bigger and deeper than I had ever known.

...You gave a love and acceptance that went way beyond that and I thank you for that. Actually, that's not entirely true. I knew my Mom loved me. You just need to know how much I love you and always did and in so many ways. Thank you for loving me.

You keep asking what my love for you means. It is authentic. It is the real thing. Much more real, if you want, than I could give you on that side. It holds life and love and laughter. It is forgiving and patient and kind. It is understanding and gentle. It comes from mind, body, soul and spirit. It is complete. I don't know what else to tell you. It is full of energy and color and compassion. It is eternal. But I don't know how to share it all with you. I have shared a little of it and it was hugely overwhelming for you.

I want you to know how much I love you. I want you to understand how huge and deep and encompassing it is. You were the world to me.... I love you more than life itself. You weren't going to write it until I pushed you. Why? I was so afraid of losing you, it was better to die than to lose you. I truly loved you more than life itself...

I told you before, that the understanding of entwined and entwined purpose goes a lot deeper on this side than it does on that side. It's like I can see the 'funnel' of it, but I don't know how to describe it or the layers of it. Maybe in time I will. But till then just accept it. It goes really deep. That is why we have such a deep "profound" love as they keep telling you. I still find it interesting that I think I was a lot more aware of that than you.

Wow! He's is getting more and more poetic as he moves along. But that was powerful for me. But then, even on this side, love can be so powerful. That is why there has been discussion about love throughout history. Thank you, Tom.

Chapter 30

Attachment

The concept of love leads into another concept that is closely related. Tom suggested that I put this chapter in the book after we had done the final editing...

He laughed saying,

There will probably be a few more chapters before the book actually gets published...this should be fun.

In psychology, issues around attachment are important so I was really interested in how Tom saw it from that side.

The line that started the whole discussion was...

I don't visit abc or xyz because there is disappointment and I don't want that to impact on them or create karma for me

Do you create karma on that side?

Oh yeah, I had to work at loving you without attachment, because attachment would create karma.

Do I need to put that into the book on lessons?

That's a good idea.

So, what did he mean?

Think of how we talked about how love was unconditional. It was important to have boundaries and respect and fair play and all that, but that the love was unconditional. You taught me how love should be unconditional for the self...that was a hard one for me. But I worked on it. And thankfully over here, I completed the lesson. But love isn't unconditional if there is attachment.

I was attached to you on that side because I was always afraid of losing you. Well not always, but it was a reoccurring thing for me. You know that.

But if I could love you unconditionally, then I could let you go and be okay with it. If you wanted to go back to being friends because it was better for us or healthier for us or something or if you decided you didn't want to be in a relationship with me for whatever reason, if I really loved you unconditionally, then I could accept that and simply allow you to be whatever you wanted to be.

But I was too attached to you for that. I wasn't mature enough for that. You were. On more than one occasion, you asked me if I needed or wanted to go back to a friendship. Or if I wanted to end the relationship. You were always so concerned about me and where I was coming from or helping me to clarify what I needed.

At first, I thought you were trying to push me away, but then you explained that you loved me so much, you just wanted what was best for me. I couldn't believe you could love me like that. I didn't love you like that. I was afraid of what would happen if I lost you.

That is unhealthy. I needed to grow up and lose my fears and my issues about not being good enough so that I could love you without attachment or love you unconditionally.

I can do that now. I love you unconditionally. I don't want to lose you or lose this connection, but if it were better for you to move onto something else without me, I would still love you, but I could let you go with love.

It is different on this side, though. If you decided to move on from our connection, I know we would connect again. I understand our connection; how entwined we are; how far we have come; how far we will still go. So that makes it okay to leave for a short while. So, in that sense it is different. There is no fear anymore and it no longer would reflect on my not being good enough. So, I would just love you, unconditionally, and let you go.

But with all of that, I had to learn unconditional love without attachment, on this side. You helped me start to engage in the lesson on that side. Together, we achieved it. Thank you.

Okay, so then what I think I am hearing is that attachment is grounded in or based on fear. When love is unconditional, there is no fear?

Yeah that sums it up.

Are there other aspects to attachment we should understand?

Attachment comes from a place of inadequacy, not being good enough, so you hang on, afraid of losing.

Love just gives without fear of losing.

I had come a long ways with all of that. What stopped me for the longest time from crossing that line of friendship was fear of rejection; which meant I could lose our friendship.

I had learned to trust you and myself and us in friendship enough that I could take that risk. I felt confident about it. I never had that with anyone else before. But then I never had that kind of friendship before either.

I was proud of myself, that took a lot of courage on my behalf. I had wanted it for so long. But I was afraid. Attachment comes from fear. You explained different types of attachment, but in my mind from this place, they all stem from fear. I no longer have those fears.

So now, my love is simply unconditional.

Okay, so I knew about the different styles of attachment in attachment theory, but I loved what Tom explained. I hope it connects for you too.

I thought Tom had finished with the chapter, I saved it and went back to our file where I type out our conversations as they occur, and he told me to come back he wasn't finished. I had to laugh, I thought we were finished. But let's continue on.

You were asking about creating karma. If we are attached to the end result, whether it be in a relationship or business or growing and developing as a human being, then we are creating karma.

That is why it is important not to have any expectations when we meditate or do any of the exercises that we do. If you are attached to the end result, then you are creating karma.

I think that often emotions are tied up in fears and when they are and when there is attachment to the results, we go to a lower vibrational frequency – that is where we started in the conversation file today.

If we can do the work, the exercises, the relationships, whatever, with diligence and come from the highest level of soul functioning, without attachment to the result, then we move forward. Our vibrational frequency increases because we are doing the work but allowing the process to be directed by a higher force, call it your higher self or God or the universe or whatever you want.

That is why Terry keeps telling you to "just allow". Do the work, don't get caught up in the results. Just allow. I think when we do whatever that way, it allows the ego/programs/and all that stuff to get out of the way and allows our higher self to come though. Yup I think that's it.

Sounded logical to me. Again, I thought Tom had finished what he wanted to share with regard to attachment. I went to have a shower, but he stopped me and said:

Attachment doesn't have to be just to people or projects or results. It can be to belief systems or emotions or reactions or situations. Anything that keeps us stuck instead of moving forward.

I was attached to the emotions I had to my Dad; I was attached to the belief that I wasn't good enough; I was attached to my fears and my programs. I think any kind of attachment works against us and creates a karmic process.

The karmic process that keeps us coming back.

Okay, now I'm finished.

I had to laugh.

Okay, great Jedi Master, thank you for the lesson.

How many times, had I been told, with regard to wanting to see Tom with intent, "just allow". The message came home one more time. I am apparently, a very slow learner. I am attached to the result. I want to be able to see Tom with intent. My attachment to the result, is getting in my way! S**t!!!

The thought, "Lessons, lessons, lessons. Will they ever end." Went through my head.

Tom laughed,

Yeah at the end of the journey when we become one with it all...till then, "its all opportunities to learn", that's what you were always saying to me...! I return it back to you.

This conversation with Tom reminded me of what I have shared with so many people over the years. I went into university to become an astro physicist, and I came out a psychologist. What a huge jump!!

Yet both avenues were ultimately connected with understanding who and why we are.

I set a goal, then made a plan, then let "God" with its infinite sense of humor guide me. I really wasn't that attached to the end result.

Another example of what Tom was explaining, that I share with people, is that North Americans tend to define themselves by their belief systems. Whereas Europeans, tend to expect their belief systems to change. Consequently, it is much easier to have discussions with Europeans than North Americans as North Americans feel the need to defend their beliefs as their beliefs define who they are. In general, my experience is that Europeans are much more open to discussion and exploration.

When it comes to attachment to emotions, I think most people can accept that if we are attached to anger or fear or resentment or whatever, it will work against us.

I think these examples reflect what Tom is saying about how attachment, whether to a result, or to a belief system, can work against us.

Chapter 31

We Can Work with Those on the Other Side

I think this is important for all of us. Once we have the strength to let down our guards and accept that there is a lot more to reality than our minimal sensory systems tell us. Once we become more aware and can go beyond the limiting, narcissistic belief that we are the only intelligent ones in the universe, then we can open up to the unlimited possibilities of life. We can start working with higher intelligences or frequencies or vibrations or dimensions.

And, once we start working with them, they can guide, teach and share what they know. Perhaps this is why the sages of old have always told us, that we have access to all the information, we simply need to learn how to open up to it.

Tom has taught me so much from the other side. Not only about him; and about me; but about out of body experiences, astral travel, healing and portals, and operating in different dimensions. It seems so old hat now, I almost forgot – feeling, hearing and seeing

Tom!!! AND, I love it, he claims we have only just begun. Why? Because he **has** only just begun.

But on the other hand, he and I, both together and individually, have worked and loved together across time, lives and dimensions. WOW! I am looking forward to having the awareness that he has of all of that.

So yes, we can obviously work with those on the other side.

People have done this for ages. Whether we call it channeling or mediumship or we look to the bible and the prophets of old or various types of shaman and medicine doctors in various cultures. This is really nothing new. Just a new experience for me in this lifetime.

Chapter 32

Can They Work with More than One Person on this Side?

When I was writing this chapter, I asked Tom should we focus on working with more than one person or connecting with more than one person? Tom suggested that we focus on just our connecting.

I have a very good friend who really loved Tom dearly. She thought the world of him. She could also see the energy that moved between us, when Tom was on this side. For the longest time she said she loved being around us just because the energy between us was so beautiful.

Suzanna also is a lot like Tom in a lot of ways. We are still forever acknowledging how many things she says and does are "pulling a Tom".

Thanks to Tom, she has connected with her father who crossed over about 40 years ago. The connection was very powerful for her and has continued to get stronger. Since that time, she has also connected with her husband, who crossed over 11 years ago; her mother-in-law with whom she was very close to and once her mother, with whom she was not close with; and her grandmother who died when she was very small but who also had 5 children with the same issues as Suzanna's – hmmmm. Suzanna regularly thanks Tom for helping her connect with her "team" on the other side.

Anyways, I started to wonder, considering that Suzanna has now made all these connections, thanks to Tom, and in consideration of how much she is like Tom, perhaps we should find out if we are meant to work together with Tom. I am always thinking along the lines of "where two or more are gathered…".

So, we booked a session with Terry. We each had an individual session and then we had a joint session where we asked:

1. Have we had past lives together?
2. What is our purpose together?
3. Should we be working together with Tom

Terry responded,

- *Tom, Suzanna and you were in one life*
- *All 3 were males*
- *The 3 musketeers*
- *You had an easy relationship, comradery*
- *There is a lot of past between you*
- *They were strong past lives*
- *You need to learn from each other*

- *Tom says she's lovely, but he prefers to work with just you - as a duo – too many hands spoil the stew*

It was actually a good session, with a tremendous amount of information, but with regard to the three questions, it was obvious that Tom didn't want to work with more than one.

On the other hand, he continues to come through to other people, including Suzanna.

I mentioned in Chapter 25, about the evening with Rudy, a friend who does all my IT computer work. One night, Rudy and I were having dinner in a restaurant. I have known him for a long time, but Tom only met him a few times. Anyways, we were sitting at the table and I was very much aware of Tom being there, as he usually was. In the middle of a sentence Rudy sat back in his chair and asked, "Wow, is that Tom? Is he really here?"

"Well, I know he is here, but I didn't know you could see him. What is it you are seeing?"

"Well, I don't really know how to explain it. I guess I am seeing his form, like it is energy. This is cool."

Yes, it definitely was cool and a lot more than that.

Another time, I was working with another good friend, Katherine, regarding her health. We were sitting in a coffee shop figuring out how to help her when she suddenly sat back in her seat and asked, "What did Tom just do to you?"

"That was a big reaction, what do you think he did?" I responded.

"I just saw him put his arm around you."

I loved it. Of course, it was continuing validation that it wasn't just me and my mind making these things up. The Cosmic Socialite, as we started to call Tom soon after he crossed over, was still making his rounds to everyone.

Anyways, a little while later, Katherine reacted again, "He did something again, I saw it. He kissed you."

Yes, in fact, he had leaned over and kissed me on the cheek. He was being "cheeky". He wanted to see if Katherine could see him, and she did. I am not sure if he was more impressed with himself or with Katherine, but ultimately it ended up being a really fun morning.

Katherine initially thought anything of this nature was in "woo woo" land. Now she connects with Tom and her guides.

My Dad and I talk several times a day, now that Mom has crossed over. He sold his home and is moving down into the new home with me. But in the meantime, he is incredibly lonely after enjoying a really good marriage for 65 years, so we talk several times a day.

One morning he phoned me and was so excited, he sounded like a 15-year-old, that just couldn't talk fast enough. He had seen Tom. He was thrilled. He loved Tom dearly and is forever asking me to ask Tom something or tell Tom something. But this particular morning, he saw Tom.

"Holly, you wouldn't believe it. He was there, just standing there, right in front of me. He had a big grin on his face as if to say, "See Pops, I can do it. I'm here." I called into the kitchen thinking at first that you must have created the image, but you were already gone. (I had left his home and come back to my home the day before.) And Tom just stayed there right in front of me. It seemed like forever!"

About a week later, I got a call from the general contractor for the new house. He phoned me three times that morning, but I was in session with clients all morning. When I got a chance to call him back, concerned that something had gone sideways with the new house, he too was like a kid full of excitement.

"Oh Holly, I couldn't wait to talk with you. You wouldn't believe what happened. I was sitting having a beer last night, thinking, Holly isn't going to like this (I have him on a protocol for a health issue) and suddenly there was this big energy beside me. I could feel it. And I knew right away who it was. I turned and asked if it was Tom. And it was. Geez, he's a big man."

I started to laugh, "Well, yeah, you are a tiny squirt compared to Tom. But how do you know you didn't just make it up."

"Well you didn't let me finish. When I went to sleep, I dreamed about him all night. First, we were at your house. We were walking around the house and he was giving me s**t because I hadn't done some things. I explained to him, that we were going to do them, we were just short of manpower right now. But I promised him we would do them.

Then we had this long philosophical discussion. He's a very wise intelligent man. I was really impressed."

"Sounds interesting, what did you talk about?"

"I haven't got a clue. I just know in the dream I was really impressed with him. Then we went over to one of the other houses I'm building, and he helped me solve a problem I was having. He's good. Then we went back to my place and had a beer. We had another really interesting philosophical conversation and you are pretty awesome."

"Okay, back up there. What did he say about me?"

"Holly, I don't have a clue. I have always been pretty impressed with you, but all I can remember is in the dream I thought, 'geez, she's more impressive than I thought'."

By this time, I was really laughing, "So you had two conversations with him and you talked about me, but you can't tell me any of it?"

"Well, normally I don't even remember my dreams, but this was pretty powerful. I thought I should tell you."

I shared with the contractor that my Dad had also had a recent experience with Tom. We laughed about how Tom was really getting around.

The Cosmic Socialite is on the prowl. I love it. Tom is having a blast and I am getting regular confirmation that this is really all happening. Actually, I hardly ever even bother to question it anymore.

Tom is great. He was a terrific guy on this side and he just keeps getting better on the other side. So, who knows what is in store. I have to leave it up to my favorite 'Jedi Master'.

Afterward

Tom says he's going to give me a break and I can finish publishing some of my other books, before we start again. My reaction was rather sarcastic, "Geez, oh great Jedi Master, thank you for the coffee break."

But truth be told, now that the self doubt and skeptic questioning is gone, I am thrilled with what I am learning and experiencing.

We both hope you gained something from reading Tom's third book.

I am adding this side note, before this book goes into publishing. I did get two more of the Entwined collection books published before he started in on his fourth book. I loved it. He just dictated the book straight to me, so it only took two days to write.

The next book, <u>Tom: The Cosmic Experience</u>, is about his experience crossing over and what happened to and with him. I sat and cried most of while he was dictating. I didn't edit most of it because it is Tom's style of talking. It was awesome. We hope you will enjoy it too.

Made in the USA
Middletown, DE
18 February 2019